Take It... It's Yours

LESTER SUMRALL

TAKE IT—IT'S YOURS
Seizing Your Spiritual Dominion

Lester Sumrall

Printed in the United States of America

Edited by Valeria Cindric

All Scripture quotations are from the King James Version of the Bible.

Formerly titled: DOMINION IS YOURS

CONTENTS

INTRODUCTION

Mathematics has its authority—its rules, formulas, and equations.

Music has its authority—its rules of harmony, time, and progression.

Christianity, too, possesses unique authority.

This book presents the principles of *dominion* and shows the power belonging to the born-again person—to the true believer living in divine harmony with Jesus Christ.

You will learn how man received dominion, how man lost dominion, and how any child of God can regain it and retain it.

Dr. Lester Sumrall

Chapter 1

UNLIMITED POTENTIAL

One of my greatest childhood thrills was holding the reins to a team of prancing, dancing horses as they pulled a wagon. Driving an automobile cannot compare to the thrill of feeling the flesh and blood of spirited steeds, ready to obey your every wish as you pull on the reins.

The greatest thrill of liberation and dominion in the world is sensing the vibrant life of Christ flooding your spirit, your mind, and your body, making you free from every tormenting habit, phobia, and fear.

God has handed you the reins of the universe and said, "Drive on victoriously through this life to the City of God." That's *dominion!*

Jesus is handing you the reins of your destiny and saying, "You hold the reins!"

Take them. What a thrill to experience the joy and confidence of knowing you hold the reins of your life. You are not under the power of any demon, disease, doctrine, or denomination. You are free to drive on furiously and gloriously to unlimited victories by the power and authority given you by the Lord Jesus Christ.

Dependency On Others

In our modern world, millions of people are totally dependent on others for their very lives. Many Christians constantly need an evangelist or pastor to support them with prayer for their physical and spiritual health. Many people seek out specialists to pry deep into their conscience, searching for solutions to deep-rooted problems. They lean on psychologists or psychiatrists to help them out of mental confusion.

Some people need pep pills to get going in the morning and tranquilizers to calm their troubled nerves at night. They don't know what it's like to wake up feeling good and retire feeling fulfilled. The joy and confidence that comes from holding the reins of life is an experience completely foreign to them.

Victories won by someone else can be lost by your own weakness later. Healings wrought by another's prayers can be lost in a moment of defeat at home or work. To realize real victory and to keep your healing, you must learn that Jesus Christ will do for you personally all that He will do for anyone else at any time or any place. You will not be completely free or permanently healed until you personally learn how to stay free by God's power.

Taking The Reins

A woman, who had previously been institution-alized, drove eleven hundred miles to have me pray for her. After praying a prayer of deliverance over this troubled woman, the spirit of God came upon her. A smile of relief replaced the tension in her face, and she gave thanks to God.

I said to her, "Now you are in command. You hold the reins of your destiny. You can stay free by your own prayers and God's power. However, you must exercise a spiritual determination to be free and realize that *you* now hold the reins! You do not have to return to me—Jesus is the same to you as He is to me."

This woman became vibrant with new hope. Her eyes, which had previously looked glassy, suddenly became alert. She realized for the first time in her life that she was now the master of her own des-tiny. I could picture her driving a Roman chariot with dashing horses moving ahead at great speed while she held the reins calm and secure!

Multitudes of people are only half blessed and half healed because they have not been taught the full truth.

It is not enough to come to the altar and say, "Lord, forgive me of my sin." The sin is gone, but your inner being is still empty. Full salvation comes when you lift your heart to God and are filled with His love, His joy, and His peace.

Once people are delivered by the strength of Christ, they must become filled with His Spirit. Then they must take the reins of power and authority in their own hands under the Lord's direction. If they will do that, they are virtually unlimited in the heights they can ascend.

Everything heaven has is open to anyone who meets God's requirements. But we must go after it. Blessing and power will not be handed to us.

When we hear about someone who is especially blessed, we say, "He's a lucky guy," or "She's a lucky person." That's untrue. Do not accept the false claims of luck. Every successful person I ever knew did everything he could to work with God and meet His requirements.

God sets the limits for those in divine relationship with Him. He says we are unlimited if we can think right and believe right in our hearts. *"As [a man] thinketh in his heart, so is he"* (Proverbs 23:7.)

The small boy with the five loaves and two fish became unlimited when he handed them to Jesus. The apostle Peter became unlimited when he stepped out of the boat onto the tempestuous waves.

When you hold the reins of your own life, you are limited only by your conception of what you can do. If you deeply believe you can do something, that is half the battle. Many people limit themselves through wrong thinking and become the victims of their own limitations.

What you can accomplish does not depend on your abilities and talents. You may say you are not naturally able to do this or that, but with God you have unlimited power.

Unlimited In God

The living, vibrant, glorious Church is unlimited. Jesus said the gates of hell could not prevail against the Church. Only the individual members who make up the Body of Christ limit the activities and victories of the Church. The Church is what we make it to be—what we believe it to be. We could say, "As the Church thinks in its heart, so is it."

As an individual member of the universal Church, you will help the Body of Christ in the earth to complete its ministry by taking your place as a free and victorious *"member in particular"* (1 Corinthians 12:2).

You are unlimited in your relationship to God. No one has reached the spiritual maximum possible in God. No one has climbed the ultimate heights. What a challenge stands before us. I look up to God as if I were a young, beginning minister, knowing there is still a world to save.

Your personal relationship to God is unlimited. You can be what you want to be. You can reach out for God's highest and best. God will call your name and say to you, "You can have anything you can conceive in your heart. Conceive it, and you can have it."

It takes time in God's presence through meditation and prayer to get God's best. If you are willing

11

to spend time with Him to discover His will for your life, no power can hold you back.

As a young man, Charles H. Spurgeon began preaching without a college or Bible school education. In a matter of a few months, he had the largest congregation in the city of London. Later, he built the Spurgeon Tabernacle that seated 5,000 people. His sermons were so powerful that the city newspapers printed them in their entirety every Monday morning. Spurgeon was a tremendous preacher of the Word of God because he gave himself completely and absolutely to the Most High. God took this young, uneducated man and used him to save thousands of people.

Discover the challenge of reaching higher than you have ever reached. God is not limited by your weakness or frailty. If He can take a Jacob and make an Israel out of him, He can do something big for you. Be unlimited in your relationship to God.

Unlimited Friendships

You are unlimited in your relationships with your fellowmen. The quantity and quality of your friendship has no bounds.

You have the number of friends you desire. If you don't have many friends, maybe you didn't go out to win many. You thought it was up to the other person to decide if he wanted to be your friend or not. That's not true. *You* are the deciding factor.

If you don't have friends, get busy! Be nice to

people, and you will never be without friends. Be unselfish, and give of yourself. Do little extra things for others, and they will be glad to call you their friend. Practice smiling a little more, and people will naturally be drawn to you.

The greatest treasures in life are friends who come at the right time with an encouraging word and a comforting touch. People who have many friends are the happiest people in the world. People who have no friends are miserable.

Learn how to develop lasting and meaningful friendships. Be a true friend to many people because the rewards are well worth the effort.

Unlimited Health And Prosperity

Health is a state of spirit—a state of the inner man. When you say, "I have health and vitality in Jesus' name," then you are on your way to being and staying healthy.

If you say, "Well, my grandpa was always sick. I'm going to be sick, too," then you'll probably get sick.

Accept unlimited health. Look up and say, "My life must shine like the stars. My life must be as beautiful and fragrant as the flowers."

Look at all of God's handiwork and say, "I will be like the rest of God's Kingdom. I will be well and strong." You will be unlimited in health and strength.

Remember, God's Word says, "As a man thinketh

13

in his heart, so is he.'' Our health has to do with our faith.

Christians are unlimited in prosperity. God blesses those who serve Him—nations or individual followers of Christ. God prospers those who recognize His power to supply all their needs.

Some Christians who had little opportunity to get a good education have become mighty in the world of business. They discovered the secret of unlimited potential in Christ.

Some people limit themselves and God by unbelief. I believe our God can do anything. If great things don't happen, don't blame God. Start searching within yourself, asking God what you can do to be unlimited.

Don't be selfish in your desire for prosperity and blessing. It is wrong to reach into the unlimited resources of God for selfish purposes. If you long to help, to love, and to bless others, God will grant you the desires of your heart.

Releasing Your Potential

God's people should be like the eagle who stretches his powerful wings and flies into the sky screaming, ''Unlimited! Unlimited!'' The great open heavens are his home, and there are no limits to how far he can go.

You can take the reins of your life and move with God into areas of unlimited blessing, anointing, faith, victory, success, friendship, and prosperity. The whole world stands before you, and you have the key. Reach for the unlimited heights for Jesus' sake, for the sake of others, and for happiness within yourself.

I don't know about you, but I am only happy in victory. I am never happy in defeat. When a friend is victorious, I am happy in his victory. When another is anointed, I am happy in his anointing.

You are the only one who can limit your life. Don't do it. Get ready for the blessings to flow. Say, "Lord, let them flow."

Release your total being to the unlimited God, and experience the true meaning of life in the Spirit.

Chapter 2

YOUR REALMS OF DOMINION

The word "dominion" originates from the Greek word *kurios*. In New Testament usage, it means lordship, inherited rulership, and sovereignty.

When we refer to human dominion, it immediately speaks to us of struggle. Human dominion does not come naturally; it is an achievement. Man must strive for dominion. This is true of everyone—from the cowboy who subdues a wild horse to the politician who is elected president.

Every human being will experience either dominion or slavery. Our enemy, the devil, seeks to enslave us, and he will never cease in his efforts. Jesus Christ, however, has already paid the full price for man's redemption from the hands of this relentless foe. He cries to the world, *"If the Son therefore shall make you free, ye shall be free indeed"* (John 8:36).

One man, Adam, lost the dominion God had given mankind; but one Man, Jesus, regained the reign. *"For if by one man's offence death reigned by one; much more they which receive abundance of grace and of the gift of righteousness shall reign in life by one, Jesus Christ"* (Romans 5:17).

The *Amplified Bible* translates the fuller meaning of the Greek as: *"shall reign as kings in life."*

If you have invited Jesus Christ into your life as Savior and Lord, the right to reign as a king in life is yours. Don't allow the devil to dominate you—you dominate him!

If you are not yet in the royal family of God, take this moment to accept Jesus as your Savior and Lord and be born into the ruling class right now. Romans 10:9-10 tells you how to be born again.

Three Realms Of Dominion

Dominion can be yours in all three realms of life: spirit, soul, and body. *"The very God of peace sanctify you wholly; and I pray God your whole spirit and soul and body be preserved blameless unto the coming of our Lord Jesus Christ"* (1 Thessalonians 5:22-23).

"God is a Spirit" (John 4:24), and man is made in the image of God. You possess a soul and a body, but you were also created with a spirit. God made your spirit to be king of your triune personality, with your soul and body under obedience to your spirit.

God gave man's spirit the ability to commune with Deity. In this realm, man is able to communicate with the divine world. Your intuition and conscience are characteristics of your spirit.

With his *spirit,* Adam walked with God in the eve-

ning and conversed with his Creator. With his spirit
he understood his limitations, such as taking the forbidden fruit from the *"tree of the knowledge of good
and evil"* (Genesis 2:17).

God made man's spirit to be the king of this tri-
unity. God made man's soul to serve and obey his
spirit. The body was made to be a slave to carry out
the wishes of the spirit directed by the soul.

As long as Adam lived in the spirit and his being
was dominated by his spirit, he had perfect fellowship with God, his environment, and his wife. Adam
was a whole person. He was well-adjusted and
happy.

When Adam rebelled and disobeyed God, his spirit
died. His actions and thoughts, now controlled by
his body and soul, were out of relationship with
God.

The Threefold Fall

In the garden, Eve responded to Satan with her
body, soul, and spirit. First John 2:16 says, *"For all
that is in the world, the lust of the flesh, and the
lust of the eyes, and the pride of life, is not of the
Father, but is of the world."*

1. *Body.* Eve *looked* upon the fruit of the tree of
the knowledge of good and evil. She *saw* that the
tree was "good for food," so she *lusted* for that
food. (See Genesis 3:6.)

2. *Soul.* The fruit was *"pleasant* to the eyes," and
Eve's soul *desired* the forbidden fruit. This unholy

19

desire meant rebellion against God. By not controlling her eyes and not looking to the Lord, Eve permitted her eyes to lust for the forbidden. This caused her downfall.

3. *Spirit*. The serpent told Eve the fruit would make her *wise*—like God. This was the sin of the spirit or *"the pride of life."*

Adam joined Eve in her rebellion, and the fall of man was complete—body, soul, and spirit. Man instantly lost his lordship and his dominion over evil and disease.

Operating In Soul Power

The devil seeks to enthrone himself in the three areas of man's *soul*—the mind, the emotions, and the will.

The mind. God wants the human mind under divine subjection. It should be directed through the human spirit by the Holy Spirit. But the devil wants to capture the human mind because the mind of man is so important. It is a perpetual battlefield. The mind suffers greater onslaughts from the powers of darkness than any other part of the human personality.

Christians are commanded to renew their minds. (See Romans 12:2.) How? With the Word of God. We are to bring every thought into captivity to the obedience of Christ. (See 2 Corinthians 10:3-5.) We are to control what our minds think. (See Philippians 4:8.)

The mind, when yielded to your human spirit that

20

is yielded to the Holy Spirit, is active and powerful. You can even have the mind of Christ! (See 1 Corinthians 2:16).

The emotions. If man does not dominate his emotions, his life will be one of defeat. Emotions dominated by a source other than God or the man himself causes stress. Stress, doctors say, is what kills man.

Having dominion gives you the ability to relax. Relaxing means releasing. Releasing gives your total being over to God for His care. When your emotions are in the care of our Almighty Lord, stress and struggle have no place in your life.

The will. No one can fully know dominion and retain stubbornness of will. The Bible speaks of those who are self-willed. (See 2 Peter 2:10.) Their natural human nature is in rulership and God's spirit of dominion is defeated and subjected to the smaller nature of man. Who is ruling your life? God's spirit of dominion or your human nature?

Spirit Dominion

The spirit of man must know dominion in order to achieve great faith and do great works. If the spirit of man does not know dominion, then no realm of his personality has hope of rulership.

God gave you dominion in your *spirit* on the day you were born-again. When your spirit is in control, you can exert dominion in your *soul*—in your mind, emotions, and will. You can exert dominion in your *body* by allowing your spirit to dictate health to the physical problems in your life.

Recently in prayer, the Lord spoke to me and asked, "Do you have dominion?"

I replied, "Yes, Lord."

"Then *look* like it!" He said.

Your appearance must not be sad, depressed, or defeated.

Again the Lord asked, "Do you have dominion?"

I replied, "Yes, Lord."

He said, "Then *talk* like it!"

Your speech reveals either dominion or defeat.

Again the Lord asked, "Do you have dominion?"

I replied, "Yes, Lord."

"Then *walk* like it!" He said.

Keep your shoulders high and walk with victory in every step!

Chapter 3

WHOSE KINGDOM IS IT ANYWAY?

Millions of men and women are held in invisible chains. They are bound by fear, by tormenting habits, and by terrible diseases that crush them. Countless numbers of people are bound by demon powers.

In primitive lands, all kinds of superstitions hold people in bondage and slavery. They are afraid day and night of unseen enemies. Their religion of demon worship, witchcraft, or spiritism causes them to live in fear.

In modern society and the western world, oppression and depression torment millions of people and hold them captive. Why is mankind enmeshed in this terrible bondage?

Designed For Dominion

God created man to be ruler of this earth. The psalmist David reveals man's lofty position and purpose as designed and decreed by his Creator: *"What* is man, that thou art mindful of him? . . . For thou hast made him a little lower than the angels, and hast crowned him with glory and honour" (Psalm 8:4-5).

The word translated "angels" in the *Authorized King James Version* of the Bible is not the Hebrew word for angels. Most good concordances and reference books will confirm that the Hebrew word in the original manuscripts is the word "elohim." *Elohim* means God. It is the word used for God in Genesis 1:1: *"In the beginning Elohim created the heaven and the earth."*

God created man just a little lower than Himself. In fact, He created man in His own image and crowned man with glory and honor. God made man to possess dominion over all the works of His hands.

"Thou madest him to have dominion over the works of thy hands; thou hast put all things under his feet: All sheep and oxen, yea, and the beasts of the field; the fowl of the air, and the fish of the sea, and whatsoever passeth through the paths of the seas" (Psalm 8:6-8).

Creatures of the air, land, and sea were placed under the supervision of man. Fish were created to swim, dogs were created to hunt, worms were created to crawl, and man was created to rule.

Even the Fall did not blot out man's original design for dominion. Throughout the centuries since creation, men have longed to fulfill their created purpose.

Created To Rule

Man was a created being made in God's image and after His likeness.

"And God said, Let us make man in our image, after our likeness: and let them have dominion over the fish of the sea, and over the fowl of the air, and over the cattle, and over all the earth, and over every creeping thing that creepeth upon the earth.

"So God created man in his own image, in the image of God created he him; male and female created he them.

"And God blessed them, and God said unto them, Be fruitful, and multiply, and replenish the earth, and subdue it: and have dominion over the fish of the sea, and over the fowl of the air, and over every living thing that moveth upon the earth" (Genesis 1:26-28).

God's love toward Adam is indicated in these words, *"God blessed them."*

The Lord indicated His desire for man to have authority on the earth when He said, *"Be fruitful and multiply."*

Man's position of dominion on this earth was forever settled when God said, *"Subdue the earth and have dominion over every living thing that liveth upon the earth."* This was man's beginning and original position of authority as ordained by God.

Fall From Glory

With such an illustrious beginning and possessing credentials of rulership from the Most High, how could man have fallen into the devil's chains of slavery?

How did man lose his place of dominion, lordship, and sovereignty?

Only the Bible supplies the answer. God's Word declares that man knowingly, willfully, and deliberately lost his freedom and became the devil's slave.

In the first place, Adam did not exercise his responsibility of lordship over the garden as God had commanded him. *"And the Lord God took the man, and put him into the garden of Eden to dress it and to keep it"* (Genesis 2:15).

The Hebrew word translated "keep" here does not mean *keep* as we use that word today. For instance, it does not mean: The Browns will *keep* our dog while we are on vacation.

This Hebrew word is more nearly like our word *guard.* If Adam was told to guard the garden, he must have known there was an enemy of God from which to guard it. But he failed to perform his God-given duty.

Adam knowingly sinned against God and delivered his kingdom and place of leadership on the earth into the hands of God's enemy. (See Luke 4:6.) The Bible says, *"Adam was not deceived"* (1 Timothy 2:14).

On the day Adam transgressed against God, fear was born in man's heart. He hid himself from God among the trees because he was afraid. That day physical mortification began, and Adam's body began to die.

Adam's spiritual nature was also affected at the time he sinned. The spirit of man fell, and he was separated from God, the Great Spirit. The highest part of his complex nature lost dominion, and man was bound by the devil's chains of slavery.

Man either has dominion, or he is under dominion. He cannot be neutral. Man was created to be dominated by no force except the Divine. He was created to be conqueror over any power or influence before him. When this divine order is not in force, the result is disaster.

When man fell, his entire kingdom—the world—fell with him. First John 5:19 declares that *"the whole world lieth in wickedness."* Utter chaos was ushered into creation. Satan became *"the prince of this world"* and the evil *"god of this world."* (See John 12:31; 16:11; 2 Corinthians 4:4.)

Man *fell* from God's grace into sin. He did not simply stumble or slip; man willfully plunged into the gutters of disgrace, despair, and disease.

Rule Regained

At this terrible collapse of man, God immediately initiated His plan to redeem man from his fallen state. God promised a Redeemer who would bruise

Satan's head. *"And I will put enmity between thee and the woman, and between thy seed and her seed; it shall bruise thy head, and thou shalt bruise his heel"* (Genesis 3:15).

Love impelled God to provide a Savior for man. Ultimately, God made the master stroke. He sent His only begotten Son, the Lord Jesus Christ, to pay the penalty for man's sin and to defeat the devil, bringing man back into a place of divine dominion.

The Bible tells us we should give thanks continually unto the Father for His wonderful plan, which *already* has taken us from Satan's hand.

"Giving thanks unto the Father, which hath made us meet to be partakers of the inheritance of the saints in light: Who hath delivered us from the power of darkness, and hath translated us into the kingdom of his dear Son: In whom we have redemption, through his blood, even the forgiveness of sins" (Colossians 1:12-14).

Adam sinned against his Creator and delivered his dominion into the hands of God's enemy. But through God's plan of redemption, the Lord Jesus Christ has restored that dominion to those who will receive it.

Jesus told His followers that dominion over the devil was His. Jesus said, *"But if I cast out devils by the Spirit of God, then the kingdom of God is come unto you. Or else how can one enter into a strong man's house, and spoil his goods, except he first bind the strong man? and then he will spoil his house"* (Matthew 12:28-29).

The strong man in this verse is the devil. Christ has dominion over him, and He gives that dominion to us. It is not something we accomplish or achieve through the brilliance of our natural minds or in our human strength. Our dominion comes directly from the Lord Jesus Christ as a gift. When we connect with Christ, He is the source of our power.

I can hold a telephone in my hand and never hear a voice until a connection is made. When I connect, I can talk around the world. It's possible to talk 12,000 miles away in a whisper. But without the connection, I cannot be heard in the next room.

Several years ago I was doing evangelistic work in the remote parts of Paraguay. I went up the Paraguay River and then rode horseback through the Grand Chaco. At one of the Indian tribes, we were told about a boy who ventured down the river into a large city far from his home.

In the evening, he saw a light shining in a local store and was fascinated by the bright bulb.

"What is that?" he asked the storekeeper.

"It is used at night to take away darkness."

"Can I buy one?" he asked.

Using all the money he had, the boy proudly bought the light bulb.

As the Indian boy journeyed home to his primitive tribe, he thought how amazed his people would be to see this bulb shine so brilliantly at night. But when he produced the bulb before his people, it would not light up. He tried and tried, but he failed to make it glow.

The boy did not know that a generator behind the store had made the power to turn on the light. The bulb had to connect with the power from the generator before it would give off light.

Jesus is the source of power in your life. With His Spirit flowing through you, your light will shine in the darkness and dominion will be yours.

Chapter 4

TAKING CHARGE OF YOUR LIFE

In our modern world, we tend to identify with large groups and avoid personal contact. People want to be associated with big organizations in order to maintain a certain distance from other individuals. Even in modern warfare, soldiers may never see the enemy. Their long-range guns and missiles make personal contact unneccessary.

There was a time in military history when men fought battles as individuals and won glory for fighting alone. For example, with only the jawbone of an ass, Samson slew a thousand of the enemies of Israel. Young David's startling confrontation with the giant Goliath is another example of individual combat. David slew the heavily armed enemy of Israel with a single stone from his slingshot.

Spiritual conflict requires individual involvement. To win in this battle, you personally must exercise dominion. When you realize that personal victory must be attained through personal conflict, you are on your way to achieving dominion.

Where can dominion be taken? How should dominion be used? You can and should exercise your Christ-given dominion in these eight areas of life.

1. The World Of Sin

Take dominion over sin. You do not have to be a slave to sin or yield to temptation.

"For sin shall not have dominion over you: for ye are not under the law, but under grace" (Romans 6:14).

Stand on that promise. In the face of temptation, say out loud, "Sin shall not have dominion over me. I choose to dominate over this temptation. I have dominion over sin according to the Word of God."

David prayed: *"Order my steps in thy word: and let not any iniquity have dominion over me"* (Psalm 119:133).

Make God's Word a part of your very being. Walk according to His Word. Then your steps will be ordered by the Lord, and you will be invested with power and authority.

2. The World Of Business And Finance

God wants His people to have the attitude of Adam toward this world. He made everything for Adam and gave him the position of dominion over His creation. God created the wealth of the world—the silver and gold are His. (See Haggai 2:8.)

Abram followed God and became Abraham, the blessed. His servant described Abraham's blessings as follows: *"And he said, I am Abraham's servant. And the Lord hath blessed my master greatly; and he is become great: and he hath given him flocks, and herds, and silver, and gold, and menservants, and maidservants, and camels, and asses"* (Genesis 24:34-35).

The Bible says, *"Abraham was very rich in cattle, in silver, and in gold"* (Genesis 13:2). Abraham was a prosperous businessman who did not allow his wealth to dominate him.

Abraham refused to allow his riches to create strife in his family or become a source of greed in his life. When the land could not support the herds of both Abraham and his nephew, Lot, because *"their substance was great,"* Abraham gave Lot first choice of grazing land. He said, *"Let there be no strife"* (Genesis 13:5-9). Abraham was not selfish.

Abraham knew that God was the source of his riches, and he paid tithes of everything he owned. (See Genesis 14:20-23.)

The New Testament declares that we who live by faith in Jesus Christ are the children of Abraham. (See Galatians 3:9,13,14,29.) Part of that blessing includes financial prosperity and dominion.

The devil seeks to dominate man's relationship to the earth in the area of finances and earthly possessions. But God wants His sons to prosper and to have an abundance for the work of the Kingdom.

A person with dominion in this area of prosperity

knows how to do his job well and how to handle money. His motives are right, and he treats his fellowman with generosity. If his motives are selfish, then he is outside the realm of dominion and is being dominated by greed.

God's people should dominate their personal finances and not be dominated *by* them. We are to exercise responsibility over the financial resources required to reach the world with the good news of the Kingdom.

3. The World Of Demons

Divine authority for the Christian extends to a realm unseen by the natural man. Dominion over devils is one of the greatest areas in which a child of God can express power.

Every disciple must know that his warfare is not physical, natural, or carnal. Paul said in Ephesians 6:12, *"For we wrestle not against flesh and blood, but against principalities, against powers, against the rulers of the darkness of this world, against spiritual wickedness in high places."*

Your battle is in the spiritual world against the rulers of darkness. An aggressive warfare is being waged on all fronts by unseen and formidable foes. The Church must exercise dominion over the powers of the spiritual world in order to reach the masses of this generation for Christ.

Christ's disciples must do what Mark 16:17 says: *"And these signs shall follow them that be-*

lieve; In my name shall they cast out devils.''

Who are these devils? They are fallen angels who fell from heaven when Lucifer exalted himself. (See Isaiah 14:12-17; Ezekiel 28:11-19.) These fallen spirits are in complete obedience to their master, Satan. Their job is to dominate humans, to cause them to rebel against God, to corrupt their thoughts, to ruin their lives, and ultimately to cause them to miss heaven.

The heathen in foreign lands are often more aware of this world of spirit beings than many Christians. This ignorance places the disciple in a losing position in the battle of the spirit world. You must know your enemy in order to defeat him.

The ultimate success or failure of the Christian disciple will not be in the visible world but in the invisible. America's military is moving away from conventional warfare on the earth and turning toward fighting in outer space. The Church, too, must move its battleground to the heavenlies against the prince and powers of the air.

The New Testament sets the divine pattern for dominion over devils. The apostles of the early Church set men and women free and wrought tremendous victories for the Kingdom of God. It must be the same today. Wherever and whenever a possessed person comes in contact with the Spirit-filled disciple, there must be a battle for deliverance.

The Lord Jesus Christ has given you authority—the right to command. He also has given you power—the right to act. May you never fail to use this delegated dominion to set men and women free by His power.

You can rejoice in the fact that the day is coming when the devil will be bound. The apostle John said in Revelation 20:1-3, *"And I saw an angel come down from heaven, having the key of the bottomless pit and a great chain in his hand. And he laid hold on the dragon, that old serpent, which is the Devil, and Satan, and bound him a thousand years, and cast him into the bottomless pit, and shut him up, and set a seal upon him, that he should deceive the nations no more, till the thousand years should be fulfilled: and after that he must be loosed a little season."*

What a glorious hour when there will be no devil, no sin, and no sickness. But until that hour, use your Christ-given dominion to paralyze Satan in every confrontation.

4. The World Of Thoughts

The human mind is the greatest arena of battle in spiritual conflict. *"For the weapons of our warfare are not carnal, but mighty through God to the pulling down of strong holds; Casting down imaginations, and every high thing that exalteth itself against the knowledge of God, and bringing into captivity every thought to the obedience of Christ"* (2 Corinthians 10:4-5).

Dominion for the disciple includes bringing every thought into captivity and making it obedient to Christ. Every thought is to be controlled and lined up with the Word of God.

When Satan injects thoughts of doubt or fear, they are to be brought into captivity and cast out with the Word of God.

When he tempts you to fear, just stop and say, *"God hath not given us the spirit of fear; but of power, and of love, and of a sound mind"* (2 Timothy 1:7).

A fearful mind is not a sound mind. Rebuke fearful thoughts. A doubtful mind is not a sound mind. Cast out doubts with the Word of Christ.

Our minds are not to be garbage containers. If they are, our thoughts will be manifested in our words and actions. Do not entertain evil thoughts. The devil may inject an unclean idea or a negative thought into your mind, but you do not have to allow it to stay. Do not pet it and toy with it. Cast it out immediately and replace it with a thought that meets all these scriptural criteria:

"Finally, brethren, whatsoever things are true, whatsoever things are honest, whatsoever things are just, whatsoever things are pure, whatsoever things are lovely, whatsoever things are of good report; if there be any virtue, and if there be any praise, think on these things" (Philippians 4:8).

If a thought is not true, honest, just, pure, lovely, and of good report, simply refuse to allow it to stay in your mind.

This is an area where every disciple can and must

assert dominion. You can bring into captivity every wild and unspiritual thought.

5. The World Of Health And Healing

Sickness and disease can be made to obey the word of power and authority. In the Great Commission Jesus said, *"These signs shall follow them that believe; In my name . . . they shall lay hands on the sick, and they shall recover"* (Mark 16:17-18).

Centuries before Christ, God declared that sickness is a curse. (See Deuteronomy 28.) Many Christians do not realize this. Some people think sickness can be a blessing in certain cases. But God calls it a curse. It is a curse that follows the broken law.

If Jesus Christ had not died for us, we would certainly come under the curse of sickness with no hope of dominion over poor health. But God's great plan of redemption redeemed us from the curse of the law, including the curse of sickness: *"Christ hath redeemed us from the curse of the law, being made a curse for us: for it is written, Cursed is every one that hangeth on a tree"* (Galatians 3:13).

When Jesus was offered on Calvary's tree as the supreme sacrifice for man's sin, the veil of the temple sectioning off the holy of holies was rent in two from top to bottom. God will never again dwell in temples made with human hands.

Today every believer is actually the temple of God. Through the power of the Holy Spirit, God's glorious presence now inhabits a living temple.

(See John 14:23; 1 Corinthians 3:16; 2 Corinthians 6:16).

God was particular about every detail of His dwelling place in the Old Testament. How much more must He be concerned about your body—the living temple for whom Christ died?

"What? know ye not that your body is the temple of the Holy Ghost which is in you, which ye have of God, and ye are not your own? For ye are bought with a price: therefore glorify God in your body, and in your spirit, which are God's" (1 Corinthians 6:19-20).

God is glorified when you have dominion over sickness and disease in your body.

Satan is the author of sickness. Adam knew no sickness until he gave Satan the authority to enter the world with all of his evil merchandise—sin, death, sickness, disease, fear, poverty, lies, and so forth.

In the area of disease, there is *authority* and *counterauthority*. The devil has power to bring disease upon you, as he did with Job. But as a Christian, you possess divine authorization to rebuke, renounce, and destroy all the power of the enemy.

You must exercise your rights, however. Sickness and disease do not automatically stay away from every believer.

Quote the source of your power. A policeman can say, "In the name of the law, stop!"

As Christ's disciple you must say, "In Jesus' name, I am healed!"

God promised that none of the diseases of Egypt would come upon His people. He revealed Himself as *Jehovah-Rapha*—"*I am the Lord thy physician*," or, "*I am the Lord that healeth thee*" (Exodus 15:26). The Old Testament is filled with the promises and provisions of God's healing power.

When Jesus came into the world, He destroyed the works of the devil—including sickness.

"*For this purpose the Son of God was manifested, that he might destroy the works of the devil*" (1 John 3:8).

Jesus said, "*Behold, I give unto you power . . . over all the power of the enemy: and nothing shall by any means hurt you*" (Luke 10:19).

Christians who are not grounded in the Word are not aware of their dominion in such a strategic area. They do not know they have the authority to resist the devil and his works. "*Resist the devil, and he will flee from you*" (James 4:7).

The devil is an expert in guerilla warfare. He sneaks in unaware, coming in camouflage. He is a deceiver, using deception to create fears, phobias, confusion, and feelings of helplessness. Man receives these terrible things, not because the devil cannot be overcome but because man listens to the devil's voice.

6. The World Of Sex

The Bible has a lot to say about the union between a man and a woman. God performed the first wedding ceremony uniting Adam and Eve. He told them to be fruitful and multiply and replenish the earth. In this way, God permitted man to join Him in divinity and in the mystery of life. Many mysteries surround mankind, but the greatest is how two protoplasmic cells unite and generate life.

Sex is the most intimate relationship between humans. And only the sexual relationship has the potential for creating an immortal soul. From the beginning, God has been very protective about sex. He addressed Himself to it very clearly in His Word. God's moral nature has never altered, and He does not change His moral standards to suit a self-indulgent generation.

Since the Garden of Eden, Satan has sought to degrade man in the area of sex. All forms of perversion, homosexuality, and moral uncleanness are contrary to God's laws of nature.

Men and women who do not exercise dominion in the area of sex cannot dominate in any area of life. Instead, they are dominated and become the victims of frustration, condemnation, regret, mental depression, and physical problems.

God wants people to be free from all abnormalities and immoral bondage. The person of dominion walks free in this area of sex.

7. The World Of Family

God ordained the family. From the beginning, He intended mankind to exercise authority in the home.

The Garden of Eden was Adam's home, and he was told to dress and guard it. Adam should not have allowed Satan to enter his home. He had the authority to keep the enemy out.

We have the authority to keep the devil out of our gardens. Take the name of Jesus and the sword of the Spirit and put Satan on the run every time you see his ugly head appearing. He has to flee.

If you have young children, or plan to have them, determine to train them up in the way they should go. God chose Abraham as the father of Israel because He knew he would teach his children the ways of righteousness. (See Genesis 18:18-19.) Many fine young parents today are bringing up their children from infancy on the milk of God's Word. They speak of the Lord in their homes at all times.

Perhaps your children are older. Maybe they were into trouble before you became knowledgeable in the things of God. God's Word says that children are a blessing from the Lord. Claim that promise. Take the name of Jesus, and break the power of the devil over your children. Then claim them for Jesus Christ, and begin to look at them in faith and love.

Your home is to be a haven of peace and love. Discipline yourself to walk in love there. Walk in the thirteenth chapter of First Corinthians, and you will walk in dominion in your family life.

8. Dominion In The World To Come

Christian dominion by the blood of the Lord Jesus Christ is not only meant for this life but for the world to come. The Word of God teaches that we will carry dominion into the world beyond.

"And the kingdom and dominion, and the greatness of the kingdom under the whole heaven, shall be given to the people of the saints of the most High, whose kingdom is an everlasting kingdom, and all dominions shall serve and obey him" (Daniel 7:27).

Kingdoms and dominion will be given to the victorious saints. We will be kings and priests forever!

"And from Jesus Christ, who is the faithful witness, and the first begotten of the dead, and the prince of the kings of the earth. Unto him that loved us, and washed us from our sins in his own blood, And hath made us kings and priests unto God and his Father; to him be glory and dominion for ever and ever. Amen" (Revelation 1:5-6).

In the future life, the victorious disciple is to be a king and a priest. This dominion includes the material realm as well as the spiritual.

Take your place of authority in every area of your life, and victory will be yours both now and in eternity.

Chapter 5

PEOPLE OF POWER

The Bible is alive with the beautiful history of people who exercised dominion on this earth. The eleventh chapter of Hebrews gives an account of the amazing use of dominion.

This chapter records that *Abel* walked in power so great *"he, being dead, yet speaketh"* (verse 4). He could not be silenced. Even today Abel's example teaches us how to give to God, for the Lord said that he made an "excellent sacrifice."

Enoch was a man of unique dominion. (See Hebrews 11:5.) He walked and communed with God on such a personal level that when it came time for him to die, he was divinely translated to heaven. Enoch left behind the testimony that he had pleased God.

Noah knew dominion. He accepted the arduous task of building the ark and saved the human race from destruction. Noah's courage, faith, and obedience made him an *"heir of righteousness"* and brought mankind under the power of the rainbow and the promise it signified. (See verse 7.)

Abraham was a great man of dominion. (See verses 8-10.) He had the courage to leave his home, country, and people and travel to an unknown land. He waged war against four kings and their armies, defeating them with his house servants of three hundred and eighteen men. (See Genesis 14.)

Abraham knew and lived dominion in every area of his life—financial, physical, and spiritual. He believed the promise and became the father of God's chosen people. Abraham's faith was the key to his life of victory.

Moses had to be a man of dominion. He led that murmuring Hebrew multitude out of Egypt's bondage, through the wilderness, and to the Promised Land. At the height of their rebellion, he pleaded for Israel before God: *"Yet now, if thou wilt forgive their sin—; and if not, blot me, I pray thee, out of thy book"* (Exodus 32:32).

Moses was a man of choice. Hebrews says that he *refused* "to be called the son of Pharaoh's daughter." He *chose* "to suffer affliction with the people of God" rather than "enjoy the pleasures of sin for a season" (verse 25). He *esteemed* "the reproach of Christ greater riches than the treasures in Egypt" (verse 26). He *forsook* Egypt, not fearing "the wrath of the king" (verse 27). He held the reins in the face of Satan and delivered God's people from the enemy's hands.

The harlot *Rahab* had the courage to believe something no one else in Jericho did. She believed that the God of Israel was *"God in heaven above, and in earth beneath"* (Joshua 2:11). She had heard how God had dried up the Red Sea for His people and defeated their enemies. Others in Jericho had heard it, too, but Rahab believed and acted. She took control of the reins of her life, saving herself and her family. (See Hebrews 11:31.)

This eleventh chapter of Hebrews lists other people who took dominion in their lives: Joshua, Gideon, Samson, David, Samuel, the prophets, and many others.

In the twelfth chapter of Hebrews, God makes a tremendous revelation: *"Wherefore seeing we also are compassed about with so great a cloud of witnesses, let us lay aside every weight, and the sin which doth so easily beset us, and let us run with patience the race that is set before us"* (Hebrews 12:1).

Lives Of Dominion

It has been my joy to know people of strength who refused to be dominated by fears or circumstances.

My mother, Betty Sumrall, was a person of dominion. I observed her life for fifty years. When the odds were great against her, she knew she would win. My mother was sure of the Word and convinced that God was performing His promises. She lived a victorious life of dominion.

For a number of years I was closely associated with Howard Carter of London, England. He was a man who knew dominion in its deepest manifestation. The British government could not break it down when they imprisoned him during World War I for being a conscientious objector. In a cramped prison cell, God gave Howard Carter a revelation of the gifts of the Spirit and their operation in the Church. Today, his message is recognized around the world. Until the end of his life, he lived victoriously with dominion.

Smith Wigglesworth of Bradford, England was another great man of dominion. I first met him at a national conference in Wales where he was the teacher and I was the evangelist. He invited me to his home, and I visited him there on a number of occasions.

Smith Wigglesworth walked in dominion no matter where he was. One time in a large restaurant in Australia, he noticed that hardly anyone bowed their heads to pray over their food. When his meal was served, Smith clinked the side of his glass with his knife, stood up, and said so everyone could hear, "Ladies and gentlemen, I have observed that almost none of you prayed over your food. You can now lay down your knife and fork, and I will pray over it for you."

With this he prayed a strong prayer. Then he said, "Thank you. Let us all eat." Later he got a number of congratulations, and two people were converted there in the restaurant. Wherever he went, Smith Wigglesworth exercised dominion.

Smith Wigglesworth told me that when he awoke

in the morning, he never asked himself how he felt. Instead, the first ten minutes of his day were used to praise and magnify God, thanking the Lord for his salvation and for the way he would be blessed that day. Few men in our generation have known the strength and dominion God placed in Smith Wigglesworth's heart.

I conducted a special conference in Stockholm, Sweden for Pastor Lewi Pethrus, a man of great spiritual strength. He had known many difficulties and had faced many problems in his life, but he was a winner. His great church—at that time the largest full-gospel church in the world—was evidence of his remarkable life of dominion in Christ.

It has been exciting for me to know people whose lives are examples of God's dominion at work. I believe multitudes of people in the world will go down in history as great men and women of dominion.

I have just learned of one such man. He is a pastor in the underground church in the Soviet Union. His story was told to me by someone who knows him personally and who visited in his home.

In the midst of spiritual darkness, I was told, this man looks like, walks like, and talks like dominion. Several times he had the opportunity to leave the country, but he chose to stay because he believed God wanted him there. He and his wife and children have remained in this communist country to preach the gospel.

This pastor has been imprisoned a total of thirteen years and has spent several of those years in

Siberia. During one term, prison officials wanted to make an example of him. They paraded this small man with the shining face before the entire prison populace saying, "This is the worst criminal in this prison."

Later, on work details, other prisoners began to make their way to him. "What terrible crime did you commit?" they wanted to know.

"I steal," he answered.

"What do you steal?"

"I steal souls from the devil!"

He then proceeded to commit that very crime upon the inquiring soul!

Seven Deadly Fears

Dominion is available to every believer. The decision is yours. Decide to be victorious in Jesus! Some people, however, refuse to exercise the dominion God has given them through Christ Jesus. They are afraid to step out and take authority over the problem areas of their lives.

Acts 1:25 says that *by transgression* Judas failed. It was not an accident. There was no weakness on God's part or an insufficient supply of power. Judas fell because he refused dominion. He yielded himself to the devil, and in so doing he lost his life.

We all know people who have refused to exercise divine dominion. Some die premature deaths. Others fail in business or permit the devil to destroy their homes.

The devil would like to attack your dominion through *fear* in these seven areas:

1. *Fear of change.* A person who refuses change grows old quickly. We say he is "set in his ways," but this literally means he refuses to change. Fear of changing jobs, fear of moving to a new location, or fear of making new friends often destroys the power of dominion. Many people could be prosperous and victorious if they were not fearful of change.

2. *Fear of people.* It is the devil's trick to make us afraid of people. Nehemiah's enemies tried to make him afraid. Nehemiah responded to their hired prophet, *"Should such a man as I flee or run and hide?"* (Nehemiah 6:11). Nehemiah knew dominion and had no fear.

Sometimes people fear their boss because he is overbearing or demanding. Other people are afraid to witness to their neighbors about their relationship with Jesus.

God told His prophet Jeremiah, *"Be not afraid of their faces: for I am with thee"* (Jeremiah 1:8). We must never fear people.

3. *Fear of the unknown.* A person can never have dominion if he fears the unknown. God commands the unknown, and His positive power is stronger than any negative force. Rest in the fact that God has His hand on tomorrow, and you need not be afraid of the unknown.

In Numbers, chapter thirteen, twelve select leaders of Israel were sent into Palestine to spy out the Land of Promise. Ten of them returned with what the Bible calls an "evil report."

They said, in effect, "The land is good, and the country is beautiful. It is rich and desirable, but giants live there." They told Moses, "We are like grasshoppers before them." (See Numbers 13:32-33.)

The nation of Israel accepted the spy's evil report. They had forgotten how God brought them out of Egypt—not through their strength but in His power. They had forgotten the miracles that took place in the desert. Now they refused the dominion that belonged to them, and they turned back into the Sinai desert. For forty years they wandered around in a waterless land until they all died. Not one of the adults who accepted that report of fear entered the Promised Land.

God had said, "The land is yours."

The devil had said, "You are too small, too weak, and too insignificant."

The Israelites obeyed the wrong source of information, and their fear of the unknown kept them from receiving God's promises.

4. *Fear of responsibilities.* No person can enjoy dominion if he fears to take on greater responsibilities. If you are willing to stay at the bottom because you cannot accept responsibility, you will never know the joys of dominion.

5. *Fear of failure.* Nothing destroys the power of dominion like the stalking fear of failure. The devil fosters this kind of fear, but the Spirit of Jesus does not know failure. When we are linked with Him, it is impossible to fail. Fear of failure comes

52

from the devil and must be destroyed before you can enjoy the rewards of dominion.

6. *Fear of added work.* You would be amazed at the millions of people who are fearful of what added work would do to them. They do not realize that while they are worrying about it, they could be accomplishing something worthwhile. Additional work brings spiritual and material growth. The devil's fears are always exaggerated and erroneous, so never be afraid of taking on added jobs.

7. *Fear of physical or mental breakdown.* Many men and women are tormented by the fear of having a breakdown. They fear the disintegration of their strength and moral courage. Job said that what he greatly feared came upon him. (See Job 3:25.)

We must rebuke all such fear and be part of that select group who have dominion. *"For God hath not given us the spirit of fear; but of power, and of love, and of a sound mind"* (2 Timothy 1:7).

Rebuke the devil, and he will flee from you. Rebuke fear, and it will flee from you. Once fear is deflected in your life, you can become the person of power God wants you to be.

Chapter 6

AUTHORIZED DEALERS

People don't like substitutes. An automobile dealer displays a sign over his business that reads, "Authorized Dealer." The sign means a consumer can expect genuine parts for his car and factory-trained mechanics to install them—and no substitutes.

In the spiritual world, Bible-believing Christians are God's "authorized dealers" of His dominion. It would be most fitting for a church to display a sign saying, "Authorized Dealer of God's Spirit and Power."

Is the victorious life of Christian dominion only for the chosen few or is it for every disciple who receives Christ as Lord and Savior?

In his epistles to the churches, the apostle Paul repeatedly spelled out the privileges and blessings belonging to each child of God.

"Blessed be the God and Father of our Lord Jesus Christ, who hath blessed us with all spiritual blessings in heavenly places in Christ" (Ephesians 1:3).

Dominion is for every believer who will accept the responsibility for exerting it.

Robbed Of Rule

After a person is born-again, the devil seeks in every way possible to hide the believer's position of authority from him. When the believer is aware of his privileges and power, Satan is completely defeated and his works destroyed.

An age-long strategy of the devil is to attack the believer in the area of confession. He knows a person will never rise above his confession. Instead of making the promises of God his confession of faith, the believer constantly confesses his sickness, faults, and weaknesses. Since a man is what he confesses himself to be, the devil uses this means to keep the believer in bondage.

Satan does not want you to confess your position of dominion in Christ or your victories by the blood of God's Son. When you make these your confession, you exert dominion, authority, and power.

Three Hindrances To Dominion

These major hindrances can keep you from experiencing victory in your rightful realm of dominion.

1. *Ignorance* is a real stumbling block to obtaining spiritual authority. A person cannot possess something he does not know he has. You could be

willed an estate worth a million dollars; yet, if you never learned about the will, you could die a pauper.

2. *Unbelief* can also keep you from entering this divinely appointed position of dominion. The children of Israel did not enter God's promised land of provision *"because of unbelief"* (Hebrews 3:19). God admonishes us to be careful lest we come short of entering His provision for the same reason. (See Hebrews 4.)

Dominion is part of God's provision. But when a believer cannot trust the promises of God and does not stand spiritually and emotionally on what God has said, it is impossible to possess true dominion.

3. *Sin* destroys man's position of dominion. When a person transgresses, he lowers himself from the limits and privileges God ordained for man in the Garden of Eden. Therefore, it is essential for a person to be cleansed by the blood of Jesus and to remain clean in order to exercise dominion.

The Spirit Of Might

The Lord Jesus told His disciples that upon His return to heaven, they would do the works that He did. *"Verily, verily, I say unto you, He that believeth on me, the works that I do shall he do also; and greater works than these shall he do; because I go unto my Father"* (John 14:12).

It is impossible to do the works of Jesus without the power of the Holy Spirit. Isaiah prophesied before the coming of the Lord Jesus that the Spirit of might would rest upon Him.

"And the spirit of the Lord shall rest upon him, the spirit of wisdom and understanding, the spirit of counsel and might, the spirit of knowledge and of the fear of the Lord" (Isaiah 11:2).

Only Christ Himself is master of all dominion in heaven and earth. Consummating His colossal achievement of world redemption, the resurrected Christ proclaimed, *"All power is given unto me in heaven and in earth"* (Matthew 28:18).

What unlimited, unrivaled, and incalculable dominion and strength are involved in that universal proclamation.

Christ is unlimited! His power is omnipotent!

His presence is omnipresent!

The believer's authority on the earth is staggering. Only Deity sets its limits, and heaven backs its God-given dominion. God wants to give every believer the Spirit of might so we can do the same works Jesus did.

The apostle Paul prayed for the believers at Colosse that they might be *"fruitful in every good work. . . . Strengthened with all might, according to his [God's] glorious power"* (Colossians 1:10-11).

Keys Of The Kingdom

Only Christ Himself can set the boundaries or categories of dominion for His disciples. These bound-

58

aries are clearly defined by the Savior and recorded in the New Testament:

"And I say also unto thee, That thou art Peter, and upon this rock I will build my church; and the gates of hell shall not prevail against it. And I will give unto thee the keys of the kingdom of heaven: and whatsoever thou shalt bind on earth shall be bound in heaven: and whatsoever thou shalt loose on earth shall be loosed in heaven" (Matthew 16:18-19). What are these keys of the Kingdom given by our Lord Jesus Christ?

Keys represent authority—dominion.

The early Church had power, and the known world was shaken by the power Christ promised His followers. *"Ye shall receive power, after that the Holy Ghost is come upon you"* (Acts 1:8).

Peter used the keys of the Kingdom when he preached the great prophetic message in Acts chapter two. The Church was birthed, and the first group of saints were filled with the Holy Spirit.

On that day Peter said: *"For the promise is unto you, and to your children, and to all that are afar off, even as many as the Lord our God shall call"* (Acts 2:39).

These words clearly reveal that this dominion was not only for the apostles. It was for the thousands of people who heard Peter's sermon on the day of Pentecost. It was for their children, and it was for those afar off—even us today.

Peter used a key of dominion at the Gate Beautiful of the temple in Jerusalem. A man lame from birth was brought daily to the gate to beg alms. Then one day things changed for him. As he looked intently upon Peter and John, he heard Peter speak these words of dominion: *"In the name of Jesus Christ of Nazareth rise up and walk"* (Acts 3:6).

Strength and dominion were the norm in the early Church.

These keys of the Kingdom are still available to the Church of Jesus Christ. The ministry of binding and loosing belongs to the Church. Whatever is bound on earth will be bound in heaven. Whatever is loosed on earth will be loosed in heaven.

Repeatedly, the New Testament emphasizes that this divine dominion was not given exclusively to the apostles.

Stephen, a deacon in the church of Jerusalem, possessed such great dominion that he did *"great wonders and miracles among the people"* (Acts 6:8).

Philip was also a deacon in the church of Jerusalem, and people were healed and set free through his ministry.

"Then Philip went down to the city of Samaria, and preached Christ unto them. And the people with one accord gave heed unto those things which Philip spake, hearing and seeing the miracles which he did. For unclean spirits, crying with loud voice, came out of many that were possessed with them: and many taken with palsies, and that were lame, were healed. And there was great joy in that city" (Acts 8:5-8).

I have always encouraged the lay members of the churches I have pastored to pray for themselves and for others, expecting answers from God. Many miracles of healing and deliverance have resulted through the prayers of simple, Spirit-filled people.

Clearly, dominion is not for a select few. It is for every disciple of the Lord Jesus Christ.

Chapter 7

WEAPONS OF VICTORY

A soldier is never sent into battle until he has a complete understanding of the weapons of his warfare. Unless a soldier knows the power of his weapons and the range of their effectiveness, he is not capable of routing the enemy and experiencing victory.

Until a Christian disciple understands the weapons of his dominion, he cannot effectively use them. The Christian must know what to do and when to do it in order to win the necessary victory.

Jesus Christ has given to His disciples all the weapons necessary for dominion on this earth. The arena of conflict, however, is in the spiritual realm.

"For we wrestle not against flesh and blood, but against principalities, against powers, against the rulers of the darkness of this world, against spiritual wickedness in high places" (Ephesians 6:12).

Weymouth's translation says our conflict is with *"the despotism, the empires, the forces that control and govern this dark world—the spiritual hosts of evil arrayed against us in the heavenly warfare."*

Our battle is not with "flesh and blood." Our battle is not with humans or denominations or organizations. Our battle is spiritual.

The conflict is spiritual and so are the weapons. *"For though we walk in the flesh, we do not war after the flesh: (For the weapons of our warfare are not carnal, but mighty through God to the pulling down of strong holds"* (2 Corinthians 10:3-4).

Learn to use the following God-given weapons of spiritual warfare.

1. The Word Of God

Every victorious Christian must learn how to use the Bible effectively. The Word of God is alive, powerful, and sharp. (See Hebrews 4:12.) The Bible is your "sword" (Ephesians 6:17). With God's Word in your heart and in your mouth, you will dominate Satan.

Revelation 1:16 pictures Jesus with a sharp two-edged sword coming out of His mouth. He used this weapon to defeat Satan in the wilderness. Jesus declared, *"It is written. . . . It is written again. . . ."* And the third time, *"Get thee hence, Satan: for it is written. . . ."* (Matthew 4:4,7,10). Like Jesus, we can use this sword with our mouths against the enemy. (See Revelation 19:15.)

The Bible is infallible and inspirational. It is inerrant in its information and supernatural in its application to daily living. But God's Word must be read and studied before it can be effective in our lives.

When I was in France on a preaching tour, a very lovely French lady came up to me and said, "I want you to know that I'm safe."

I must have looked confused because she went on to explain, "I bought a Bible yesterday and put it in my mailbox."

"In your mailbox?" I repeated.

She said, "The devil will have to pass by the mailbox to get to me. With the Bible inside it, he can't hurt me anymore."

I said, "You better sit down and let me tell you a little more about the Bible. We don't believe in using God's Word like a lucky charm. The Word of God must be read and studied in order to be effective in your life. You must get it into your heart. God's Word only works on the inside of the believer, not in the mailbox."

In my personal life the Bible has been a true guide in every crisis. When God wants to lead me in a new direction, He directs me through His Word. The Bible is my sourcebook for truth. When I want to know what is right and wrong, I refer to what the Bible says about the matter.

You can be a mighty man or woman of God by giving the Word first place in your life. If you feed your spirit daily on the Word of God, you will grow spiritually. (See 1 Peter 2:2.) Your spirit, strong and well-nourished, will dominate your being. Rather than being ruled by the outward man, the inner man will rule over your mind, will, emotions, and flesh. You will know your God and do exploits in His name.

2. The Name Of Jesus

Jesus gave the Church His Name. The Name of Jesus is above every name. At that Name, beings in heaven, in earth, and under the earth must bow. (See Philippians 2:9-11.) That Name is dominion!

Before He was crucified, Jesus spoke to His followers of the soon-coming day when He would give them the power of attorney to use His exalted Name. They would use it in prayer. (See John 16:23-24.)

Jesus spoke of His followers doing the works that He did, and greater works, because He was going unto His Father. In the next breath He said, *"Whatsoever ye shall ask in my name, that will I do, that the Father may be glorified in the Son. If ye shall ask any thing in my name, I will do it"* (John 14:13-14).

After His death, burial, and resurrection, and before He ascended to sit down at the right hand of the Father, Jesus told His disciples to *"Go . . . and teach all nations"* (Matthew 28:19).

The gospel of Mark records the signs that would follow the believers as they carried out Jesus' orders: *"In my name shall they cast out devils . . . they shall speak with new tongues . . . they shall take up serpents . . . if they drink any deadly thing, it shall not hurt them . . . they shall lay hands on the sick, and they shall recover"* (Mark 16:15-18).

That's dominion! And it's all in His Name! Every soldier of the cross who walks in victory and dominion knows that he possesses this mighty weapon—and he knows how to use it.

3. Faith

Without dynamic faith born in the heart at conversion and nourished through the Word of God, a believer cannot successfully engage in battle with demon power and win.

When Jesus came down from the mount where He was gloriously transfigured, He was met with the news that His disciples had been unable to cast the devil out of a certain man's lunatic son. His first reaction to the report was, *"Oh faithless generation."*

The devil departed, of course, at Jesus' command.

His disciples asked Jesus, *"Why could not we cast him out?"*

"Because of your unbelief," Jesus replied. *"If you have faith as a grain of mustard seed, ye shall say unto this mountain, Remove hence to yonder place; and it shall remove; and nothing shall be impossible unto you"* (Matthew 17:14-20).

When a person is challenged by temptation, disease, or the devil, his faith must constantly come into focus. He must have faith to command God's power.

When God told Abraham He was going to destroy

67

Sodom and Gomorrah, Abraham reasoned with God. He stood before the Lord and said, *"Wilt thou also destroy the righteous with the wicked? Peradventure there be fifty righteous within the city: wilt thou also destroy and not spare the place for the fifty righteous that are therein? That be far from thee to do after this manner, to slay the righteous with the wicked. . . . Shall not the Judge of all the earth do right?"* (Genesis 18:23-25).

God agreed to Abraham's request and said He would not destroy those wicked cities for the sake of fifty righteous people. Abraham decreased the number of the righteous to forty-five, then forty, then thirty, then twenty, and finally to ten. Each time the Lord was willing to meet Abraham's conditions.

The true power of faith never has been fully utilized by man. God is still waiting for heroes of faith to use the divine dominion He gave to Adam in the Garden of Eden.

In the New Testament Church, it was the force of faith that caused Peter to turn to the body of a dead woman and say, *"Tabitha, arise"* (Acts 9:40). It was by faith that the apostle Paul commanded the spirit of divination to come out of the fortune-telling damsel. (See Acts 16:18.)

Faith is the key that unlocks the generosity and strength of God. Faith pleases God, but *"without faith it is impossible to please him"* (Hebrews 11:6).

Faith has been called the eye that sees the invisible, the ear that hears the inaudible, the hand that feels the intangible, and the power that works the impossible.

Jesus said, *"All things are possible to him that believeth"* (Mark 9:23).

Faith works by the spoken word. Saying and believing go together, as Jesus explained: *"Whosoever shall say unto this mountain, Be thou removed, and be thou cast into the sea; and shall not doubt in his heart, but shall believe that those things which he saith shall come to pass; he shall have whatsoever he saith"* (Mark 11:23).

Faith is an act. Martin Luther gave this view of faith: "It is a busy, active, living reality that does not ask, 'What shall I do?' but before it has time to ask, it is up and doing."

David believed Goliath would be defeated, so he hurled a stone at his head. *Faith acts.*

Faith is a way of life—a walk with God. The great miracles that characterized Smith Wigglesworth's ministry were the result of his close walk with God. He talked with God so often and for so long that when Smith made a request it was easy for God to understand. The tendency of many is to walk so far from God that it is not possible to hear Him when He speaks. But the person of dominion will walk with God and live out his faith. Living faith, the life of God, will flow from his innermost being.

How do you get faith? The rule is simply this: *"Faith cometh by hearing, and hearing by the word of God"* (Romans 10:17).

The Word alone is the source of faith. But the

Word will not build faith unless it becomes a part of your very being. Jesus said, *"If ye abide in me, and my words abide in you, ye shall ask what ye will, and it shall be done unto you"* (John 15:7).

4. Prayer

Throughout history every outstanding man and woman of God has been a person of prayer. Prayer is one of the Christian disciple's most powerful weapons. In prayer, the believer receives the infilling of divine energy. After Jesus had prayed and fasted for forty days, He victoriously defeated Satan single-handedly in the greatest spiritual struggle ever recorded.

The prayer closet is actually the *council chamber* where divine commands are issued. In order to possess great dominion, you must constantly return to the Master to receive instructions from Him.

The prayer closet is the *heart-study place*. This is not where the mind learns, it's where the heart becomes instructive. In prayer we learn about God, His blessings, and His anointings.

Jesus told Peter, *"Flesh and blood hath not revealed it unto thee, but my Father which is in heaven"* (Matthew 16:17). We learn more in an hour of devotion and prayer than in many hours of searching libraries and seeking out man's wisdom. Divine revelation is brought into focus in the prayer closet. You won't find it anywhere else. Prayer is the key that unlocks the treasures of God.

Prayer is power.

Elijah demonstrated the dominion of prayer when he called upon God to send rain upon the land. The New Testament points out that Elijah was a man like we are. The difference is, he knew how to pray.

The early Church prayed, and the place where they were assembled together was shaken. (See Acts 4:31.)

Paul and Silas prayed and sang songs in the inner cell of a Philippian jail at midnight. The strength of their prayer shook the jail itself and resulted in the salvation of the jailer. (See Acts 16:25-34.)

The act of praying generates omnipotence. Prayer gives the frail human reed unshakable strength.

If you do not know how to pray, you do not know the power of God. Prayer is the most talked about, discussed, and the least used power available to mankind.

Oil, undiscovered, is an untapped resource. Coal, not mined, is an untapped source of power. But the greatest source of untapped power and resource is prayer. All that prayer can do has never yet been defined. This tremendous source of power has never been fully researched or developed.

In his article, "Man the Unknown" published in *Reader's Digest,* Dr. Alexis Carrel said: "As a physician, I have seen men, after all other therapy had failed, lifted out of disease and melancholy by the serene effort of prayer. It is the only power in the world that seems to overcome the so-called 'laws of nature.'"

Through personal communication with the Creator, you can do things you could never do before. Pray without ceasing, and you will know dominion in your life. Continual communion with the Commander assures victory.

5. Action

Dominion means *to do.* Dominion is an *act* and not an idea. God does not give power to the inactive. Jesus said, *"He that believeth on me, the works that I do shall he do also"* (John 14:12).

Throughout history, those who possessed dominion were men and women of action. God told Moses to stretch forth his rod, and the waters of the Red Sea rolled back, making a path for the children of Israel. (See Exodus 14.)

Jesus told a man with a withered hand, *"Stretch forth thine hand"* (Matthew 12:13). Jesus did the rest. The man's hand was restored whole like his other hand.

In most instances in God's Word, action was necessary before dominion was realized. The children of Israel had to march around Jericho before the walls collapsed. Naaman had to dip seven times in Jordan before his leprosy was cleansed.

Works alone are not sufficient for salvation or dominion. But some action is necessary—even vital.

Paul reminded the Corinthian Christians that there is work to do for the Kingdom of God. *"For we are labourers together with God"* (1 Corinthians 3:9).

In the second chapter of James, even stronger language is employed. *"What doth it profit, my brethren, though a man say he hath faith, and have not works? Can faith save him . . . Even so faith, if it hath not works, is dead, being alone"* (verses 14,17).

The word translated "works" here implies action. One translation reads, *"Faith without corresponding actions is dead."*

It is not enough to know God's will—you must do it. *"Not with eyeservice, as menpleasers; but as the servants of Christ, doing the will of God from the heart"* (Ephesians 6:6).

Having money is not enough. Knowing you have it is not enough. You could know you had money in the bank and still go hungry and cold. You must go to the bank, withdraw some cash from your account, and spend it for food and warm clothing.

So it is with Christian dominion. Before it pays off with bountiful blessings, dominion must be put in force with action on the part of the believer.

Dominion is an instrument to better enable the disciple to work for God and to obey His commandments.

God's commandments have always been: *Go. Do. Give. Work.*

By using the pertinent weapons of dominion, any believer can be a triumphant Christian. Therefore, I urge you to stand up, use the instrument God has given you, and have dominion with Christ. Be an overcomer and a blesser of mankind all the days of your life.

Chapter 8

TAKING YOUR RIGHTFUL POSITION

God's Word says, *"My people are destroyed for lack of knowledge"* (Hosea 4:6). Without knowledge of your true relationship with God, you cannot possess dominion over the many conflicts of life.

Suppose someone kidnaps a king's only son, the crown prince of the realm. Later, the child is abandoned. A beggar finds and adopts the boy, having no idea of his identity. Now the child of the king eats beggar's refuse, clothes himself in filthy rags, and begs from house to house.

But suppose the king knows the young prince by a birthmark that establishes his identity beyond question. The royal father never gives up his search for the prince.

One day the king hears that a child resembling his son lives in a distant city with a beggar. Arriving at the beggar's hovel, the king examines the child and finds him to be his son. The crown prince is washed and groomed. He is given a robe, a ring, and a place of authority in the kingdom.

Although he was the son of the king, the crown prince had lived for years like a beggar because he did not know who he was. He did not know his position of dominion.

Many Christians today are like this prince. They belong to Christ and are sons of God, yet the devil keeps them in ignorance so they will not realize their divine right of dominion. Once they understand the basis of their dominion in Christ, they live a new life attendant with power and victories.

It is imperative that you know—and *know* that you know—your rights as a follower of the Lord Jesus Christ. You are entitled to dominion.

These steps gleaned from God's Word will help you take dominion in your personal life.

Recognize Your Source Of Power

In Ephesians 1:17-23, Paul prayed a prayer for Christians. He specifically requested that God grant them *"the spirit of wisdom and revelation"* concerning certain vital truths. He knew they needed to understand some things. One thing he wanted them to know was: *"What is the exceeding greatness of his power to us-ward who believe"* (Ephesians 1:19).

You and I must understand the exceeding greatness of His power directed toward us who believe. We must know the exceeding greatness of God's power flowing through us.

Paul's prayer given by the Holy Spirit describes

this mighty strength directed toward us as:

"According to the working of his mighty power, which he wrought in Christ, when he raised him from the dead, and set him at his own right hand in the heavenly places, Far above all principality, and power, and might, and dominion, and every name that is named, not only in this world, but also in that which is to come: And hath put all things under his feet, and gave him to be the head over all things to the church, which is his body, the fulness of him that filleth all in all" (Ephesians 1:19-23).

Recognize your source of power!

Your power comes directly from headquarters—and headquarters is in heaven.

We have a daily source of strength and power the world knows nothing about. The world cannot tap it. The only way to get into this power is to get into Jesus. The only way to get into Jesus is to believe in Him. The only way to believe in Him is to accept Him as your Lord and Savior. (See Romans 10:9-10.) When Jesus becomes Lord of your life, this exceedingly great power is yours.

Recognize your source. And recognize what is not your source. Your source is not the human mind. Your source is not human strength. Your source is God!

Recognize Your Need For The Church

The most powerful living organism on the earth

today is the Church—the very Body of Christ. Jesus Christ is the Head of this Body.

"And he is the head of the body, the church: who is the beginning, the firstborn from the dead; that in all things he might have the preeminence" (Colossians 1:18).

"Now ye are the body of Christ, and members in particular" (1 Corinthians 12:27).

Jesus Himself described the irresistible strength of the Body.

"I will build my church; and the gates of hell shall not prevail against it" (Matthew 16:18).

For many centuries the Church did not fully recognize her indomitable power. But you and I are living in a day when this powerful organism is waking up ready to arise and shine as the prophet Isaiah foretold. (See Isaiah 60.)

We are the Body of Christ, and we must accept our spiritual authority. We must realize that the gates of hell cannot prevail against the Church. As we move together, nothing can stand before us. We can change anything we want to change on the face of this earth.

Recognize your relationship to the Church, and be closely related to Christ's Body of believers. You cannot neglect the Body of Christ and be strong in the Lord. Your relationship with other believers is very important.

Some people say, "It doesn't matter if I go to church or not." That is a lie from the devil.

Believers minister to each other. People sitting in

the pews have encouraged me as I preached. Something in me rose up as I looked at them. If they had stayed home, I wouldn't have gotten that inspiration or received that blessing. At times I've been so blessed shaking someone's hand at church that I didn't want to let go.

People who stay home are selfish. You can never grow in God and be selfish.

"Even when we were dead in sins, [God] hath quickened us together with Christ, (by grace ye are saved;) And hath raised us up together, and made us sit together in heavenly places in Christ Jesus" (Ephesians 2:5-6).

We are to sit together in spiritual places in Christ Jesus.

A good friend of mine, who held a responsible position with a large firm, was asked to transfer to another area of the country. He was offered a much higher salary.

This man traveled to the area and searched for a church he liked. When he could not find one, he returned and said to his boss, "I don't want the new position."

His superior said, "Why don't you want the job? Isn't it good?"

He said, "I suppose it is. But I can't find a church I want to worship in there. So I don't want the job."

His boss could not understand. This man refused the advancement because he couldn't find a church where he and his family could worship, learn, grow, fellowship, and work.

Thousands of Christians have backslidden because they moved to places where they couldn't find a church that met their spiritual needs. Almost every day I hear someone say, "I can't find a good church where I live."

I say, "Why did you move there?"

The most important thing in life is your spirit, soul, and body—not your pocketbook. The most important thing for your children is to have a good church where they are taught God's Word.

Recognize your relationship with the living Body of Christ. That is the path of victory and dominion.

Identify Your Enemy

If you don't know who your enemy is, you won't be able to win a victory. You won't know where to deliver a blow.

If you think your enemy is your wife, your husband, your children, or the church, you will never be able to win a victory. Striking out at the wrong foe only makes matters worse.

Moffat's translation describes our enemies as *"the angelic rulers, the angelic authorities, the potentates of the dark present, the spirit-forces of evil in the heavenly sphere"* (Ephesians 6:12).

First identify your enemy. Satan is the enemy of God and the enemy of God's creation, mankind. When Satan strikes at the human personality, it is imperative to recognize the source of the trouble.

Instead of getting grouchy and grumpy, get into

a state of prayer and say, "Let me see here. My wife is a sweet person, so it is not her. This is from the devil. I am going to resist him."

Close your fist and say, "Satan, in the name of Jesus Christ of Nazareth, I command you to take your hands off my marriage. Get out of my house. And get out of here *now*!"

By saying this, you will have identified your enemy. You will have successfully stopped his tactics, and you won't be fighting against your family.

Know Your Enemy's Weakness

The devil is completely defeated by the Lord Jesus Christ. He can't do anything against Jesus. No devil or demon anywhere can combat the Holy Spirit. The early apostles brought great fear to demons who cried and ran away from the disciples' presence.

Any true believer can rebuke the devil today. He still has to flee when Christians resist him. *"Submit yourselves therefore to God. Resist the devil, and he will flee from you"* (James 4:7).

We do not necessarily have to fight the devil. We can simply remind him of Calvary where the Lord Jesus Christ defeated him. Remind him of his complete defeat and of his ultimate destiny—hell. Tell the devil, "Don't you know what is ahead of you? Don't you know where you are going to endure eternity?" Then tell him that you know he is a defeated foe.

Satan is limited. He is limited by his fallen state. (At one time he was an archangel.) Christ's resurrection cut him short and stripped from him the keys of hell and of death. (See Revelation 1:18.)

Satan has a bruised head that cannot be healed. In the Garden of Eden, God foretold that the Seed of the woman was coming. (See Genesis 3:15.) This Child of a virgin would bruise Satan's head and break Satan's lordship. The devil and all his cohorts know that Jesus Christ fulfilled this prophecy and brought them *"to nought"* (1 Corinthians 2:6-8).

All evil spirits, who were brought to nothing by the Lord of Glory, fear and tremble before any believer with the power, the anointing, and the authority of Jesus Christ.

Do not talk about how big and strong the devil is. If you do, you will believe it. Instead, remind him that he has already lost the war. Remind him he is under your feet and you are walking on top of him. (See Ephesians 1:19-23.) He understands that.

Stay Ready For Battle

We have an enemy whose key strategy is to keep the Christian away from his place of authority and spiritual power. Satan tries to keep us "off base."

Be aware of his tactics. Immediately resist and refuse to accept any of the following states Satan may try to put upon you.

Vexation. If Satan can keep you in an agitated state, you cannot cast out devils. If he can keep

82

you angry with someone, you cannot heal the sick.

Learn to recognize the enemy's working in your life. Keep your mind on Jesus, and you will have perfect peace.

Depression. If the devil can get you depressed, you are not effective in the Kingdom. You cannot minister to others when your heart is weighed down.

Depression can come from many sources—from your home, at work, or in your body. Events can take place that make life seem hopeless.

You can get depressed listening to the news. If that happens, turn off the news and read two or three chapters in the Bible. News reports don't give a clear picture of things anyway. Most reporters give their ideas about things, and their ideas sometimes come from perverted minds.

Confusion. If the devil can get you confused, you will not be effective in God's Kingdom. Life is simple. You only have to make one decision at a time. If you ask God for wisdom, He will help you make each decision without confusion. But once you make a decision don't keep making it all day long. Don't take the dress back to the store forty times. Keep it when you buy it.

Stop for a moment and say, "My name is Sam Jones. My address is so-and-so. I work at such-and-such a place. I am married to Mary Jones, and I have so many children. I am saved and filled with the Holy Spirit. I belong to such-and-such church. Devil, I don't need to know much else, so get out of my way."

The devil does not want you to be ready for battle. He wants you in a state of confusion. If you are, you are not prepared to resist him.

You don't have to live in a state of confusion! The devil is a liar, and there is victory in Jesus!

Anything that is not clear today will be clear tomorrow. Rejoice in today, and God will bring peace and clarity out of confusion.

Selfishness. If the devil can get you to be self-centered and keep you looking at yourself, you will not be ready to be used by God. You will be constantly wondering, "How am I getting along? What can I do for myself? Me. . . . My. . . . Me. . . . My. . . ."

Be Christ-centered. Say, "Lord, I am out to win souls, and I don't mean maybe! Devil, we're coming after them. They belong to Jesus, and you can't have them!"

The devil would like Christians to be so self-centered about their business and homes that they lose the vision for saving the world.

Many years ago when I was in China, a Chinese communist told me, "You have more missionaries than we have communists in China—but we are going to take China. Do you know why?"

I asked, "Why?"

He said, "You teach people to give ten percent. We teach them to give one hundred percent. I give everything to the party. We are going to win."

I just stared at him not knowing what to say. But

I can assure you that as long as you are self-centered you are ineffective. Get lost in the great love of God, and lose your self-centeredness. Love the world. Love the people of your community. Then you are ready to defeat the devil.

Recognize The Power Of Praise

Jesus said, *"Whatsoever ye shall bind on earth shall be bound in heaven: and whatsoever ye shall loose on earth shall be loosed in heaven. . . . For where two or three are gathered together in my name, there am I in the midst of them"* (Matthew 18:18-20).

The devil is subject to the believer's *faith,* and he cannot overcome it.

The devil is subject to the believer's *authority,* and he must submit to it.

The devil is subject to the believer's *rights,* and he can't take them away.

The devil is subject to the *words* a believer speaks, and he must obey. If the believer tells the devil to go, he must go!

One of the most dramatic and powerful demonstrations of dominion is *singing.*

The entire nation of Israel sang a song of triumph as they crossed the Red Sea. *"The Lord is my strength and song. . . ."* (Exodus 15).

Deborah and Barak sang a song of victory. (See Judges 5.)

Paul and Silas sang in the Philippian jail. Their

shackles fell off and the gates flung open. (See Acts 16:25-26.)

Almost all nations have anthems that arouse national pride in their people. Armies sing military songs as they march into war.

New Testament believers are told: *"Be filled with the Spirit; speaking to yourselves in psalms and hymns and spiritual songs, singing and making melody in your heart to the Lord"* (Ephesians 5:18-19).

God wants us to be glad and sing songs of victory. Go throughout life singing, "Jesus already has won! The Church already is victorious!"

If the devil says something about it, stop him by saying, "Shut up, in Jesus' name. We have already won the battle!"

There is victory in Jesus. Whatever you need, He has already won for you. Just claim what is yours in His name.

If you are sick, say, "I thank You, Father, that Jesus has obtained my healing. I receive it now in His name. Thank You. I have it now."

Remember! *You are what God says you are! You can do what God says you can do!*

Chapter 9

SUPREME AUTHORITY

No other person ever asserted dominion like the Lord Jesus Christ. He knew divine dominion. *"For in him dwelleth all the fulness of the Godhead bodily"* (Colossians 2:9).

Our Lord Jesus had dominion in every stage of his life.

His virgin birth, first spoken of in the Garden of Eden, had been prophesied through the prophet Isaiah 750 years before the Babe lay in the manger.

"Therefore the Lord himself shall give you a sign; Behold, a virgin shall conceive, and bear a son, and shall call his name Immanuel" (Isaiah 7:14).

His supernatural birth transgressed the laws of nature.

"And the angel answered and said unto her, The Holy Ghost shall come upon thee, and the power of the Highest shall overshadow thee: therefore also that holy thing which shall be born of thee shall be called the Son of God" (Luke 1:35).

The One who had lived through all eternity—the

One who was with God and was God—the One by whom all things were made—became flesh and dwelt among us. (See John 1:1-4,14.)

Through the power of the Holy Spirit, Jesus entered an earthly body so He could defeat Satan for us.

"Wherefore when he cometh into the world, he saith, Sacrifice and offering thou wouldest not, but a body hast thou prepared me: In burnt offerings and sacrifices for sin thou hast had no pleasure. Then said I, Lo, I come (in the volume of the book it is written of me,) to do thy will, O God" (Hebrews 10:5-7).

His supernatural entry into the world set the stage for a life of dominion.

At twelve years of age, Jesus showed amazing wisdom. He not only quizzed the shrewd lawyers in Jerusalem, but He answered their questions as well. The authority of His words and answers amazed the intellectuals of Jerusalem.

"And it came to pass, that after three days they found him in the temple, sitting in the midst of the doctors, both hearing them, and asking them questions. And all that heard him were astonished at his understanding and answers" (Luke 2:46-47).

Authority Over Temptation

Immediately after Jesus was baptized by John, the Spirit of God descended upon Him, and the Father said, *"This is my beloved Son, in whom I am well pleased"* (Matthew 3:17). Jesus then went forth into the wilderness to exercise dominion over the temptations of the devil.

Jesus met temptations of the spirit, temptations of the soul, and physical temptations while living in a body of flesh. He defeated them all with the power of the written Word of God and the word of His testimony.

"It is written," He powerfully declared, *"Man shall not live by bread alone, but by every word that proceedeth out of the mouth of God"* (Matthew 4:4).

Dominion Over Tradition

Jesus' teaching was not like any the people of His day had ever heard, and they recognized the difference immediately. What made His teaching different?

"And it came to pass, when Jesus had ended these sayings, the people were astonished at his doctrine: For he taught them as one having authority, and not as the scribes" (Matthew 7:28-29).

The *authority* in His teaching made the difference.

The Spirit of might was upon Jesus, and everyone stood back and watched while He worked.

"And Jesus went into the temple of God, and cast out all them that sold and bought in the temple, and overthrew the tables of the moneychangers, and the seats of them that sold doves, And said unto them, It is written, My house shall be called the

house of prayer; but ye have made it a den of thieves.

"And the blind and the lame came to him in the temple; and he healed them. And when the chief priests and scribes saw the wonderful things that he did, and the children crying in the temple, and saying, Hosanna to the Son of David; they were sore displeased" (Matthew 21:12-15).

After Jesus loosed the temple of God from men's traditions, the blind and the lame came to him; and He healed them.

Tradition is a terrible, destructive influence that can bury you. You can get so steeped in tradition that you say, "It's always been done that way, and we are always going to do it that way." If you are bound by tradition, God cannot move in your life in a new way to help and bless you.

Dominion Over Nature

At the beginning of Christ's public ministry, His first miracle turned spring water into sparkling, delicious wine. (See John 2:1-11.) This was accomplished without the fermentation process of nature.

"This beginning of miracles did Jesus in Cana of Galilee, and manifested forth his glory; and his disciples believed on him" (John 2:11).

Those around Jesus were suddenly aware of His dominion as they observed nature obeying Him!

Christ showed Himself to be the master of nature

90

by walking on the Sea of Galilee. His disciples were troubled and amazed at such dominion.

"And in the fourth watch of the night Jesus went unto them, walking on the sea. And when the disciples saw him walking on the sea, they were troubled" (Matthew 14:25-26).

Jesus further demonstrated His power over nature by calming the tempestuous sea with a spoken word.

"And there arose a great storm of wind, and the waves beat into the ship, so that it was now full. And he was in the hinder part of the ship, asleep on a pillow: and they awake him, and say unto him, Master, carest thou not that we perish?

"And he arose, and rebuked the wind, and said unto the sea, Peace, be still. And the wind ceased, and there was a great calm. And he said unto them, Why are ye so fearful? how is it that ye have no faith?

"And they feared exceedingly, and said one to another, What manner of man is this, that even the wind and the sea obey him?" (Mark 4:37-41).

God created the earth with a perfect weather system, but Satan brought about devastating upheaval. As a result, storms and winds have driven man—who was created to rule the world—to seek protection from the elements.

When Jesus rebuked the storm and spoke to the sea, they obeyed His words. Believers have that same dominion over the elements, and the Lord expects us to use our authority. In the ship Jesus rebuked His disciples for being fearful and faithless.

Dominion Over Disease And Sickness

"How God anointed Jesus of Nazareth with the Holy Ghost and with power: who went about doing good, and healing all that were oppressed of the devil; for God was with him" (Acts 10:38).

Throughout His earthly walk, Jesus went about doing good and healing. He exercised complete dominion over the disease and sickness Satan had brought to mankind.

A Roman centurion—a man who understood authority—came to Jesus on behalf of his paralyzed servant who was sick at home. When Jesus said, "I will come and heal him," the centurion answered:

"Lord, I am not worthy that thou shouldest come under my roof: but speak the word only, and my servant shall be healed. For I am a man under authority, having soldiers under me: and I say to this man, Go, and he goeth; and to another, Come, and he cometh; and to my servant, Do this, and he doeth it.

"When Jesus heard it, he marvelled, and said to them that followed, Verily I say unto you, I have not found so great faith, no, not in Israel. . . .

"And Jesus said unto the centurion, Go thy way; and as thou hast believed, so be it done unto thee. And his servant was healed in the selfsame hour" (Matthew 8:3-10,13).

Christ healed that servant with the spoken word of authority. The Roman officer's faith drew a commendation from Jesus. By contrast, Jesus' disciples had not recognized His authority, and Jesus rebuked them for their lack of faith. (See Mark 4:40.)

Many scriptures reveal that Jesus Christ always exercised authority over sickness and disease. He never failed to heal those brought to Him.

"When the even was come, they brought unto him many that were possessed with devils: and he cast out the spirits with his word, and healed all that were sick" (Matthew 8:16).

The Lord Jesus never revealed any evidence of fear over the forces of nature or disease. He dominated them completely.

Dominion Over Demons And Death

From the beginning of His ministry, the Lord Jesus demonstrated His *power over evil spirits* of all kinds.

The following is only one of several recorded instances. In this passage demons recognized Jesus and feared Him. They raged against their victim in a final effort to remain, but the words of faith from Jesus caused them to leave and set the man free. People could see the authority and power of Jesus over the evil spirit.

"And in the synagogue there was a man, which had a spirit of an unclean devil, and cried out with a loud voice, saying, Let us alone; what have we to do with thee, thou Jesus of Nazareth? art thou

come to destroy us? I know thee who thou art; the Holy One of God.

"And Jesus rebuked him, saying, Hold thy peace, and come out of him. And when the devil had thrown him in the midst, he came out of him, and hurt him not.

"And they were all amazed, and spake among themselves, saying, What a word is this! for with authority and power he commandeth the unclean spirits and they come out" (Luke 4:33-36).

The demoniac of Gadara had 2000 or more such demons. Mary Magdalene had seven. Some people had spirits of blindness, others had spirits of dumbness, and many had unclean spirits; but they all yielded to Christ's dominion.

Death had to yield to Christ's dominion, too. The Lord Jesus asserted His authority over the powers of death by raising the dead.

He raised a girl from the dead while she was still in her home. (See Mark 5.)

He raised a boy from the dead as he lay on his funeral bier. (See Luke 7:11-15.)

He raised Lazarus after he had been dead for four days. (See John 11.)

Christ possessed dominion over death and over all the power of the enemy.

The Lord Of Glory

The apostle Paul called the demonic powers in the world system *"princes of this world, that come to nought"* (1 Corinthians 2:6).

Then he spoke of the glorious plan of God that brought them to nothing.

"But we speak the wisdom of God in a mystery, even the hidden wisdom, which God ordained before the world unto our glory: Which none of the princes of this world knew: for had they known it, they would not have crucified the Lord of glory" (1 Corinthians 2:7-8).

The devil and his cohorts played right into the plan of God and brought about their own doom when they crucified Jesus. In His death, burial, and resurrection, Jesus completely destroyed the power of the enemy and delivered mankind.

"Forasmuch then as the children are partakers of flesh and blood, he also himself likewise took part of the same; that through death he might destroy him that had the power of death, that is, the devil; And deliver them who through fear of death were all their lifetime subject to bondage" (Hebrews 2:14-15).

When Jesus appeared to John the Revelator on the Isle of Patmos, He said, *"I am he that liveth, and was dead; and, behold, I am alive for evermore . . . and have the keys of hell and of death"* (Revelation 1:18). Keys represent authority.

After His resurrection, Jesus remained with His followers for forty days. He concluded His earthly ministry by declaring, *"All power is given unto me in heaven and in earth"* (Matthew 28:18).

That is *supreme dominion!* But Jesus did not stop

there. Because He was given all power, Jesus was able to add the command to go to all the nations, teaching and baptizing in the name of the Father, Son, and Holy Spirit. (See Matthew 28:19.)

No person on record has revealed and taught dominion like the Lord Jesus. The Bible says of Him, *"In whom are hid all the treasures of wisdom and knowledge"* (Colossians 2:3).

Jesus delegated His authority on the earth to His Body, the Church.

Mark's account of the momentous delegation of authority declares that Jesus said, *"And these signs shall follow them that believe; in my name shall they cast out devils; they shall speak with new tongues; they shall take up serpents; and if they drink any deadly thing, it shall not hurt them; they shall lay hands on the sick, and they shall recover"* (Mark 16:17-18).

Dominion over demons, over disease, and over all the power of the devil was and is now restored to Christ's Body, the Church, *in His name!*

Chapter 10

EXERCISING COLLECTIVE DOMINION

Satan not only tries to steal personal dominion and individual authority, but he works hard to enslave entire communities, cities, and nations. He does this through lying philosophies taught in secular schools, books, media, and even in some churches. Empires are destroyed through lies that lead to weakness.

Pagan religions enslave entire nations. From the highest to the lowest the people bow down in fear before idols and superstitions. These nations abound in fear, poverty, disease, and all that Satan brought with him into the earth.

But God offers collective dominion to those who will accept it!

Communities Of Dominion

A community can exercise collective dominion if a strong spiritual leader is in control. Abraham's pilgrims became a large community. He had 318 armed servants who defeated and destroyed four kings and their armies. This battle was the first recorded conflict in the Bible.

How exciting it must have been to have lived in that community. General Abraham himself trained and equipped the army. He taught his men they could conquer in spite of great odds because they had added power—Jehovah God's power!

There are cities in the world where the saints of God have taken dominion over entire areas.

This was true in Zion, Illinois for many years. It was founded as a Christian city, and for a long time no cigarettes or alcoholic beverages were permitted to be sold. People could sense the Spirit of the Lord as they entered the area.

So-called "evangelical cities" have a very different "feeling" than pagan cities. For example, I found Calcutta, India, with its millions of Hindu gods, to be one of the most depressing cities on the face of the earth. The city is named after Cali, a female goddess. Cali is a fierce devil. When you see her image at the great temple, her tongue sticks out about six inches wide and eight inches long. This goddess demands blood. Her followers bring goats to the temple and cut their throats, letting the blood flow into a groove under the hideous idol. Her devotees then splash their faces and drink the hot goat blood. I have been there several times, and it is sickening. The entire area reeks of Satan. Sin, sickness, poverty, and death reign. Anyone can see it and feel it.

On the other hand, there are several cities in the United States today that are especially possessed by

God's people and His Spirit. Many great works of the Kingdom of God go forth from them. When you enter the city, the very atmosphere warms your whole being.

I know a city affected by the dominion of the saints. One morning the pastor of a small church in that town walked by the corner bar on his way to the post office. He had been going by that bar for years. But that morning he placed his hand on the old brick wall and cursed the bar in the same manner his Master had done to a fig tree two thousand years before.

In a few weeks, the bar closed. Someone reopened it, but it closed again. The pastor had forgotten how he had prayed until the Spirit of the Lord reminded him.

A young woman, who was youth director of the church, was impressed by the Spirit to claim the bar for God's service. After much hard work, the former bar reopened as an evangelical outreach center for youth.

A few doors down the street was an old pool hall. The youth workers decided they needed the building for their ministry, so they began to pray. Within a few months, the pool hall went out of business and a recreation center for restless young people was opened in its place. This small town is being possessed by the people of God who are taking dominion over the works of Satan.

Jesus wept over Jerusalem, the largest city in Israel at that time. Today, we should weep over the great cities of our land lest they become throne rooms of the devil's power.

No power can stand before the living Church. The Lord Jesus promised that even the gates of hell could not stop His Church. Let's advance on the big cities. Let's possess our communities for Christ.

The City Of God

Abraham looked for a city whose builder and maker is God (Hebrews 11:10). And so do we. *"But ye are come unto mount Sion, and unto the city of the living God, the heavenly Jerusalem"* (Hebrews 12:22).

God's Word paints a picture of a city where divine dominion reigns supreme. The only things missing are the curses and problems Satan brought with him when he usurped man's rule.

"And I saw a new heaven and a new earth: for the first heaven and the first earth were passed away; and there was no more sea. And I John saw the holy city, new Jerusalem, coming down from God out of heaven, prepared as a bride adorned for her husband.

"And I heard a great voice out of heaven saying, Behold, the tabernacle of God is with men, and he will dwell with them, and they shall be his people, and God himself shall be with them, and be their God.

"And God shall wipe away all tears from their eyes; and there shall be no more death, neither sor-

row, nor crying, neither shall there be any more pain: for the former things are passed away'' (Revelation 21:1-4).

God's glory fills the holy city. Every citizen of the heavenly city is a victor. Every person is a redeemed and immortal soul.

"And he carried me away in the spirit to a great and high mountain, and shewed me that great city, the holy Jerusalem, descending out of heaven from God, Having the glory of God. . . . And I saw no temple therein: for the Lord God Almighty and the Lamb are the temple of it. And the city had no need of the sun, neither of the moon, to shine in it: for the glory of God did lighten it, and the Lamb is the light thereof" (Revelation 21:10-11,22-23).

God's glory fills His temple in the earth today. We, the Church, are that living temple. When we take the dominion that is now ours, His glory enlightens the places we possess. For the Lamb is our light indeed.

Nations Of Dominion

When Israel honored God, no enemy could stand against her. If they came before her one way, they fled before her seven ways. The Red Sea's waters rolled back to let the nation of Israel through. Jericho's walls tumbled before the people of Israel. Canaan's inhabitants were no match for Israel's God. The All-Sufficient One was her provider, and the Lord of Hosts was her healer.

The Most High God was Israel's strength and shield. It was His desire that everyone should look at her dominion over all the power of the enemy and say, "There is a God in Israel!" Then, like Rahab, they would want to know Him as their God.

But nations, like individuals, must decide to serve God. Israel's choices were set before her when God said, *"I call heaven and earth to record this day against you, that I have set before you life and death, blessing and cursing: therefore choose life, that both thou and thy seed may live"* (Deuteronomy 30:19).

Ancient Israel forsook her God to worship devils. (See Deuteronomy 32:17.) When she did, she gave up her dominion. Her inhabitants were dispersed throughout the earth, leaving her land idle and desolate for hundreds of years.

The United States of America is one of the most unique nations of all times. Early settlers came to her shores seeking religious freedom. In-depth studies into Virginia's earliest visitors from Europe reveal startling facts of the leading of the Spirit of God.

We have been known to the world as a Christian nation. "In God We Trust" is stamped on our money. "One nation, under God" is recited in our pledge of allegiance to the flag.

Even today the gospel goes forth from this nation as no other in history. The majority of all missionary work is supported from this nation by the sacrificial giving of millions of Christians.

Who Is Responsible?

Freedom to worship; freedom to assemble; freedom of speech; freedom of the press—all these are birthrights often unappreciated by those of us born within America's domain.

Our nation has blessed Israel and known the blessing that results according to God's Word. (See Genesis 12:3.)

In 1956, however, America took a position against Israel. Our commanders demanded that France and Britain remove their troops from the Suez Canal Zone. Israel was forced to give back to Egypt the entire Sinai that Israeli soldiers had taken in battle. America cut off relations with Israel, and no planes were permitted to land and no ships could dock. My family and I lived in Jerusalem at that time, and it was France that fed us.

Since that time, America has lost ground and glory in Korea, Vietnam, Cuba, Africa, Asia, and South America.

God has placed the state of a nation into the hands of His people who dwell there. *"If my people, which are called by my name, shall humble themselves, and pray, and seek my face, and turn from their wicked ways; then will I hear from heaven, and will forgive their sin, and will heal their land"* (2 Chronicles 7:14).

The people of God living in a land can exercise their collective dominion. They can hold the reins of the nation in their hands.

Christians everywhere should practice the following New Testament admonition to pray for the leaders of their government. *"I exhort therefore, that, first of all, supplications, prayers, intercessions, and giving of thanks, be made for all men; For kings, and for all that are in authority; that we may lead a quiet and peaceable life in all godliness and honesty. For this is good and acceptable in the sight of God our Saviour; Who will have all men to be saved, and to come unto the knowledge of the truth"* (1 Timothy 2:1-4).

The Church in the United States is responsible before God for this nation. Let us rise up and take our dominion on behalf of our country—and on behalf of the countless millions of lost humanity whom God would have to be saved. The gospel must continue to go forth freely from the United States of America.

Chapter 11

POWER AGAINST POWER

Today's generation is a *power* generation. New power drugs, power weapons and power machines are developed every year. We have power politics with men struggling for position. The world is drunk on power—*dominion*. Man loves power—from the popping of an inch-long firecracker to the blasting of an atomic bomb. The whole world is seeking greater power.

We dig for the hidden power of coal that has lain dormant for centuries. It is transformed into power to move engines and heat furnaces.

We drive machinery deep into the bowels of the earth to suck out oil and gas for our mechanized age. Our society is dependent on electric power. Without it cities are paralyzed and modern conveniences are obsolete.

When man took hold of atomic power to harness and release it, two cities in Japan were disintegrated. Since that day, the world has lived in fear of a nuclear holocaust.

In the air above us, radio waves speed around the world at 180,000 miles per second. That's seven times around the world in one second!

At our television station here in South Bend, Indiana, we have a link-up with a satellite. A television broadcast image can leave Virginia or North Carolina or California—or any other place producing an up-link—and travel 22,300 miles above the earth to the satellite and back down through the down-link in South Bend in less than a second. You can barely bat your eye before it is up and back down again.

Our world is power conscious, but power can be used in two ways—constructively or destructively. Man has to decide which way to use power.

The Power Of Sin

The most destructive force in the universe is sin. It is the greatest destroyer of mankind.

Organized crime, an evil that has hurt many people, operates through the power of sin. Newscasts are replete with reports of murders in small hamlets and large cities—men killing men, women killing women, children killing children. Mankind seems to have lost respect for human life and human dignity.

Sin causes all murder, thefts, and adultery. Drunkenness, gambling, and cheating is the result of sin. All moral uncleanness comes from sin. Sin has power.

No human can tackle the power of sin and win over it. Your human power cannot stand up against sin's power because the devil is the originator of sin. He is the head captain of everyone who steals, kills, or destroys. *"The thief cometh not, but for to steal, and to kill, and to destroy"* (John 10:10). Natural human strength is no match for Satan's power.

The Bible describes Satan in his original state. In heaven he was *"full of wisdom, and perfect in beauty"* (Ezekiel 28:12). He was adorned with every perfect stone that glitters—diamonds, rubies, and other precious stones (verse 13).

But Lucifer turned his God-given will against God. Instead of choosing to worship God, he rebelled against his Creator and fell from his place of beauty and glory. Isaiah 14:12-15 tells the terrible story. Jesus told His disciples how He had beheld Satan as lightning fall from heaven (Luke 10:18).

Isaiah 14:12 identifies him as the one who weakened the nations. Any nation weakened by Satan's power is eventually destroyed. Lucifer is described as the one who "made the earth to tremble" (Isaiah 14:16). Every time there is war, revolution, or turmoil, the devil is the force behind it. He "shakes kingdoms" and creates havoc throughout the world (verse 17).

A few days after World War II was over, I went to Europe. In London I saw the buildings where I had lived completely destroyed. The Bible college where I had taught was gone. In France whole cities where I had preached many times were nothing but rubble. I just stood there and cried, "Oh, God! Oh, God!"

Any time you see destruction, there is a sinister

personality close by—the devil. His ministry is one of destruction.

The Power Of Our Savior

God's Word tells us of a far greater power than Satan. *"But we preach Christ crucified, unto the Jews a stumblingblock, and unto the Greeks foolishness; But unto them which are called, both Jews and Greeks, Christ the power of God, and the wisdom of God"* (1 Corinthians 1:23-24).

What is Christ? Christ is the power of God! *"For I am not ashamed of the gospel of Christ: for it is the power of God unto salvation to every one that believeth"* (Romans 1:16).

The gospel is the power of God. The gospel we preach is not words, not notions, not philosophic ideas—it is the power of God! *"But as many as received him, to them gave he power to become the sons of God, even to them that believe on his name"* (John 1:12).

When we receive Christ into our hearts, something happens to us. To as many as receive Him, He gives power.

"But ye shall receive power, after that the Holy Ghost is come upon you: and ye shall be witnesses unto me both in Jerusalem, and in all Judaea, and in Samaria, and unto the uttermost part of the earth" (Acts 1:8).

We receive power after the Holy Spirit comes upon us. Aren't you glad for that?

When I think of power against power, it reminds me of a dam. To stop a river from running, you dam it up and make a lake out of it. Which is stronger—the water flowing down the river or the dam? If the dam has been properly engineered, it can stand against the force of the water. Flood waters rise against it, but the dam remains firmly in place. Its staying power is stronger than the moving power—so the moving power can do nothing but back off.

When it is power against power, the weaker power must back off. When it is power against power, one power will always supersede.

God's power will always supersede the power of evil when we exercise it. God wants to bring His children to the place where we know and exercise our God-given power.

When Satan comes against God's people, he should find a dam of faith holding him back. We should say, "Back off, waters of evil, we're here to stay. We're here to hold you back and to tell you how far you can go."

Steel can be made so tough that steel won't cut steel. But a little diamond put into a vice can cut through the strongest piece of steel. Why? It's force against force—power against power. Something has to give.

The steel says, "I am tough."

The diamond says, "Yes, but I am tougher. You yield to me. I am the boss."

Jesus was talking about power against power when He said, *"But if I cast out devils by the Spirit of God, then the kingdom of God is come unto you. Or else how can one enter into a strong man's house, and spoil his goods, except he first bind the strong man? and then he will spoil his house"* (Matthew 12:28-29).

The devil may be tough, but we are tougher. He may be strong, but we are stronger. We have to know this principle, however, before it will be effective in our lives. We must live with the power and divine authority of God.

In Indonesia some years ago I met a little Dutch missionary from Holland. When she first went back into the mountains of Indonesia to preach the gospel, the local witch doctor told her to leave. He said she was in his territory.

This little missionary said, "You don't have any territory. I am going to stay."

He said, "No! I don't like other witch doctors coming in here. I respect other witch doctors. I don't go into their places, and I don't want them in mine."

She said, "I'm no witch doctor."

He said, "You act like one."

They quarreled for some time. Finally, the witch doctor said, "Let's see who has the most power. The one who has less power, let that one leave."

The missionary agreed.

The witch doctor said, "Let's meet on a certain day and ask everybody to come."

On that day, the whole village came to see what was going to happen. They thought two witch doctors were going to have a contest to decide who would be boss of that community.

The young woman missionary and the witch doctor stepped onto a platform.

The witch doctor looked at her and said, "Do something."

She didn't know what to do, so she said, "You do something."

He lay down on the floor before all the people and became stiff as a board. Very slowly, the powers of levitation caught him, and he rose up ankle high, then knee high, until he floated in the air.

The people were amazed. Surely he was the most powerful, they said.

The Dutch girl thought, "I know I can't float. I guess I'll have to leave."

God said, "No, you don't!"

She said, "Well, what am I going to do?"

God said, "Get him down! Put your foot on his belly and push him down."

So she walked over to him, pulled up her long skirt a little, put her foot on his belly, and pushed him against the floor.

Then God said, "Cast the devil out of him!"

So she said, "Come out of him in the name of Jesus!"

The devil came out at her command. When the man came to his senses, he didn't know where he was. He had been so possessed by the devil that he hadn't been in his right mind. He didn't even know the contest was taking place.

He said, "Where am I? What am I doing here? What is this all about?"

She reached over and pulled him up to a sitting position. She told him what had happened, and he received Jesus as his Savior. She laid hands on him, and he received the Holy Spirit.

As a result, the missionary was made the administrator of the town, and the former witch doctor became the mayor. When they had a community meeting, she sat in a chair beside him, giving advice only when she felt he needed help. Soon the village became known as the Refugee Town. Anyone who had received Jesus and was being persecuted could come there and live with them.

In our everyday lives, we face problems and situations that are power against power. It is up to us to decide who is the winner.

Jesus Christ is the winner, and God wants each of us to be winners, too. He has made it possible for us always to triumph in Christ Jesus. God wants everyone of us to know and confess His mighty power. You cannot confess defeat and at the same time give Jesus authority in your life. You must confess victory in Jesus' name.

Until the end of this age, it will be power against power. But God's Word has settled forever the fact that the greater power resides in the believer—not in the world.

"Ye are of God, little children, and have overcome them: because greater is he that is in you, than he that is in the world" (1 John 4:4).

The "them" we "have overcome" are demons and evil spirits. The greater One who is in us is Jesus through the power of the Holy Spirit. The devil is "he that is in the world."

Jesus is the greater One. He is in you. You are not a loser. You are a winner. So take your place of dominion—it's yours!

Chapter 12

WINNING THE PRIZE

All new model automobiles are tested to see if they can perform efficiently when the rubber meets the road. Your life is the same. When the rubber meets the road, what kind of a person are you? Are you a quitter? Are you a grumbler? Or are you an endurer?

James 1:12 says, *"Blessed is the man that endures temptation: for when he is tried, he shall receive the crown of life, which the Lord hath promised to them that love him."*

The word "blessed" is related to joy. We could say, "Joyful is the man who endures temptation." The joy comes on the other end—not so much in the midst of the temptation. Joy results from enduring. The trying or the testing reveals your true character.

How To Resist Temptation

Resisting temptation is like any other aspect of the

Christian life—certain principles must be followed in order for you to be successful at it. If you put these guidelines into practice, you will have victory over temptation.

1. *Set your heart.* Your heart must be set against the source of your temptation. If you think one way one day and another way the next, then you are not stable. (See James 1:8.) Any time you don't know what is right, you're going to do the wrong thing.

"Daniel purposed in his heart that he would not defile himself with the portion of the king's meat" (Daniel 1:8). Daniel knew what was right, and he said, "I purpose in my heart. I will not defile myself." How could the best food in the world be defiled? In Babylon, all the meat was offered up to idols before it was eaten. Daniel would have been worshipping the devil if he had eaten it. He purposed in his heart, he stood his ground, and God honored him for it.

2. *Be careful who you listen to.* Other people may try to influence you to be unfaithful to God.

Job's wife said to him, *"Dost thou still retain thine integrity?"* (Job 2:9). Someone today might ask, "Do you still go to church after all that has happened to you?"

Job's wife also suggested that he *"curse God and die,"* but Job responded to her in the right way. "You're talking like a foolish woman!" he replied.

Listening to wrong counsel can get you into trouble and cause you to sin. But Job refused to take his wife's advice. The Bible says, *"In all this did not*

Job sin with his lips" (verse 10). Get your direction from God and avoid the counsel of the ungodly.

3. *Refuse to have companionship with worldly people.* Ungodly companions can turn your heart away from God and His ways.

Proverbs 4:14 says, *"Enter not into the path of the wicked and go not in the way of evil men."*

If your companions are wicked people, then you're going to become like them. If you like to be with your old cronies, you are going to fall back into your old ways.

If you want to live in glory and victory, you must choose godly companions. In order to walk with God, you must walk with God's people.

4. *Be prepared to face temptation.* If you're going to be victorious in your Christian living, you need to be prepared spiritually.

Ephesians 6:13 says, *"Take unto you the whole armour of God, that ye may be able to withstand in the evil day, and having done all, to stand. Stand therefore."* When you have done everything, keep on standing.

Why Bother To Resist?

Why should we shun evil and resist temptation? Because Christ commands us to live in a state of perfection. We may not be able to live in ultimate perfection, but we can experience perfection of love and an attitude of duty toward God. Jesus said, *"Be ye therefore perfect, even as your Father which is in heaven is perfect"* (Matthew 5:48).

If you're going to live a victorious life, don't move toward degradation—move toward perfection. Be a better person today than you were yesterday. Be more mature in your Christian walk this week than you were last week.

The apostle Paul said, *"I keep under my body, and bring it into subjection: lest that by any means, when I have preached to others, I myself should be a castaway"* (1 Corinthians 9:27).

Plenty of people can tell you how to live right yet not do it themselves. Every sinner in town can give you a one-hour sermon on how to live right while he goes on swearing, committing adultery, and getting drunk.

Paul says, "If I don't keep my body under control and bring it under subjection, then when I have talked to others, I myself will be a castaway. I must not only talk to you, but I must live it myself."

Two ministers recently telephoned and asked me to pray for them. Although they both have large churches and successful ministries, these pastors were depressed. How can they minister joy to their people if they are in a state of depression?

Don't instruct others, and then become a castaway. You have to shun temptation in Jesus' name.

Avoiding Mistakes

The apostle Paul said, *"All these things happened unto them for ensamples: and they are written for our admonition"* (1 Corinthians 10:11). If you see what's happened to others by their transgressions, that will keep you from falling. The things that happened to people throughout the Old Testament were written for our admonition.

Mr. Howard Carter, my teacher and mentor, said, "Don't ever think of beginning where I did. I've been there; you begin where I quit. You begin here and then go on." He would rebuke me sometimes and say, "I've seen young men who had great privileges but who never amounted to anything. What are you going to do?"

"I'm going to do my best," I'd say.

"You better do more than that!" was his reply. For years he prodded me into believing for God's best.

When we see the shipwreck of others, we don't have to take the same boat. When we see the discouragement of others, we don't have to jump in that pool of despondency. When we see others stumbling along the pathway of life, we don't have to take that same road. There is a way of victory for every one of us.

When you read about the sins of Samson and David, you can avoid making the same mistakes. Their trials and temptations are written in the Bible so you won't fall into the same traps.

James 4:7 shows us the strength and dominion we have over sin. He says, *"Submit yourselves therefore to God. Resist the devil, and he will flee from you.''* Many of us know the last part of the verse, but we leave off the conditional part.

First, submit yourself to God by surrendering your life completely to Him. After you have done that, then you have a right to tell the devil to leave. When you've submitted to God and you command Satan to leave, he has to go.

If you're not submitted to God, the devil does not have to obey you. If you're living in sin, you can't say, "Get away from me devil!" He won't pay any attention to you. He'll just hug you a little tighter! But if you're living under God's discipline, the devil cannot touch you.

Running To Win

How do we become strong in the Lord and in the power of His might? First Corinthians 9:24 says, *"Know ye not that they which run in a race run all, but one receiveth the prize? So run, that ye may obtain.''* We are victors when we put our energy into positive action.

This verse does not say if you sit in a rocking chair and rock along, you'll win a prize. It does not say if you sit in your lazyboy and watch television, you will receive a crown. The Bible says, "Run!" If we are going to be mighty men and women of God, we need to get into a spiritual training program. Those who run receive the prize, so don't quit.

Paul must have attended the Olympic games when he visited Athens. He saw the young men—

powerful, strong, and determined—training for the Olympics. As he watched them, Paul knew that any of those athletes who were striving for mastery or perfection were temperate in their lifestyle. *"Every man that striveth for the mastery is temperate in all things"* (1 Corinthians 9:25).

Athletes in training don't stay up late at night or gorge themselves on junk food. Anyone who strives for the mastery is temperate in all areas of life. If you are seeking to be a master, God says you must be temperate. A disciplined life is the key to victory.

"Let us lay aside every weight, and the sin which doth so easily beset us, and let us run with patience the race that is set before us" (Hebrews 12:1). This is the secret to being a winner. Lay aside every sin that is weighing you down and keeping you from running the race to victory.

The rewards of a victorious life are worth all the effort you put into running the race. The man who endures temptation will receive *"the crown of life"* (James 1:12). The trial of your faith is *"more precious than gold"* (1 Peter 1:7).

"To him that overcometh will I grant to sit with me in my throne, even as I also overcame, and am set down with my Father in his throne" (Revelation 3:21).

When temptation comes, kick it out of the way and march forward. Live for Jesus and love God. If you truly love God and are committed to Him, you will be promoted by the Father to a higher grade in His Kingdom.

In this life, we receive earthly rewards for the good we do. But we also live for the reward in heaven that will be given to all who have received eternal life. Do not let the devil discourage you. If he can get you to stay home from church, if he can get you to stop witnessing, if he can get you to stop praying, if he can get you to stop reading the Bible, he's the winner and you are the loser.

Pray this prayer with me: *Father, thank You for victorious living. The devil is defeated and destroyed. I am a winner on the side of Jesus, and I will be victorious. Anoint me in faith and courage to endure to the end and win the crown of life. In Jesus' name, amen.*

Dominion over Satan and the world has been given to you, so *take it—it's yours.*